MW01231422

Little
Excel 4
Book
Windows Edition

Tim Toyoshima

Peachpit Press
Berkeley, California

The Little Excel 4 Book, Windows Edition

Tim Toyoshima

Peachpit Press, Inc.
2414 Sixth Street
Berkeley, California 94710
(800) 283.9444
(510) 548.4393
(510) 548.5991 fax

Cover design: Ted Mader + Associates

ISBN 0-938151-63-0

0 9 8 7 6 5 4 3 2 1
Printed and bound in the United States of America

PRINTED ON RECYCLED PAPER

To my wife, Nanette,
and my son, Nicholas

Acknowledgements

Although my name is on the cover of this book, many other people also put a lot of work into this book. Thank you all:

- *Jesse Berst* for giving me the opportunity to do this project and lending his editorial touch.

- *Ted Nace* for being everything I could hope for in a publisher.

- *Byron Canfield* for his design and production wizardary, and Paula Richards, for her valued design comments and suggestions.

- *Anne Edmondson* for editorial support.

- *Mark Dodge* for his help planning and for his technical editing of the Excel version 3 book.

- *Scott Dunn* for his input on the book design, *Kathy Underwood* for final copy-editing, *Steve Whitney* for his input on Chapter 5, *Steve Kahn* for his stock market expertese, AND *Bonita Sargeant, Barry Potter,* and *Lori White* for their moral support.

- My wife *Nanette Knox Toyoshima* for being patient and understanding and my son *Nicholas* for being a great baby.

Contents

CHAPTER 1: Getting Results   1
   Surveying the territory 2
   Staying on friendly terms with Excel 5

CHAPTER 2: Learning the Essentials   11
   Selecting cells 12
   Moving within a worksheet 14
   Finding the tools you want 15

CHAPTER 3: Setting Up a Worksheet   23
   Entering text 24
   Entering numbers 32
   Entering formulas 37

CHAPTER 4: Editing and Formatting a Worksheet   47
   Editing cell contents 48
   Moving and copying cell contents 49
   Deleting and inserting cells 51
   Formatting worksheets 52
   Finding, replacing, and spellchecking 66
   Fast Formatting 71

CHAPTER 5: Creating Charts and Worksheet Graphics   79
   Creating charts 80
   Using worksheet graphics 100

CHAPTER 6: Printing   **107**

    Selecting a printer .108

    Selecting the print area 109

    Switching to Print Preview 109

    Setting up page layout 111

    Repeating titles on every page 118

    Setting page breaks 119

    Printing documents 120

CHAPTER 7: Linking Information   **121**

    Creating a linked copy of cells 122

    Creating formulas using linked references .128

    Linking to other applications 129

    Working with multiple worksheets 133

    Editing multiple worksheets 137

CHAPTER 8: Organizing Information   **139**

    Using a database 140

    Using an outline 148

CHAPTER 9: Speeding Up with Macros   **153**

    Recording macros .154

    Running and assigning macros 155

Index   **165**

CHAPTER 1

GETTING RESULTS

Everyone wants results fast. As a Microsoft Excel user, you want to enter data, analyze it, and present it right away. This book was created just for you. I'll cut through Excel's massive list of features and give you the essential skills to put information in a worksheet, analyze it, organize it, and present it. No mumbo jumbo. Just the facts.

This first chapter gets you off to a quick start by giving you:

■ An overview of the Excel screen and worksheets— the base from which you do all your work

■ A practical, proven approach for working efficiently in Excel

SURVEYING THE TERRITORY

Before you speed off to create a worksheet, you need to get your bearings. Otherwise, you may run headfirst into a wall. To avoid headaches later on, read this section to get oriented with worksheets and the Excel screen.

What's a worksheet?

Software applications are often patterned after real-life tools. Excel's *worksheets* imitate the paper ledgers used by accountants (Figure 1-1). The *rows* and *columns* intersect to form *cells* that hold data.

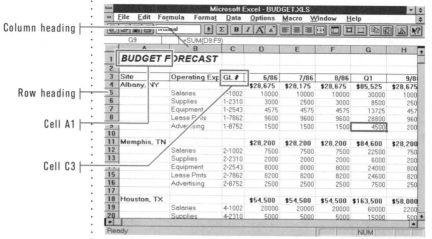

Figure 1-1. *Software imitating life: Excel worksheets are modeled after an accountant's paper ledger.*

Each column and row has a *heading*. Columns have letter headings (in alphabetical order), such as A, B, C, and so on. Rows have number headings. You refer to a cell by its *cell reference*, which is simply its column letter and row number. For example, the first cell in a worksheet is A1 (column A, row 1). Likewise, cell C3 refers to the intersection of column C and row 3.

You can enter two types of information in a cell: constants and formulas. A *constant* is a value that won't change unless you edit it or replace it. Constants can be text, numbers, dates, or times. On the other hand, a *formula* depends on other values and uses them to calculate a new value. For example, the Excel formula =A1+C3 adds the values from cells A1 and C3, and displays the result.

Getting your bearings

If you've used other Windows programs, you already know a lot about Excel. You choose commands and size the windows just as you would in any other Windows program. However, the Excel screen has special features you may not recognize.

Within Excel's *application window*, you can have three types of *document windows*: worksheets, charts, and macro sheets (Figure 1-2). *Worksheets* hold and display your data and formulas as well as graphic objects. *Charts* use the data from a worksheet and display it as a graph. *Macro sheets* store macros, which you can use to combine a series of actions to automate your work. You'll learn about all these types of documents in the chapters to come.

The *title bar* for the application window displays the name of the program (Microsoft Excel). The title bar for the document window displays the active document's filename.

Mighty mouse

There are at least two ways to execute almost any Excel command—with the mouse or with the keyboard. This book shows you only the mouse method because it's the easiest to learn and usually the fastest to use.

The mouse relieves you from having to memorize keystrokes so you can concentrate more on what you're doing, not on how to do it.

So if you want to get results fast, start by working with the mouse. After you get a handle on the concepts, then try some keyboard shortcuts.

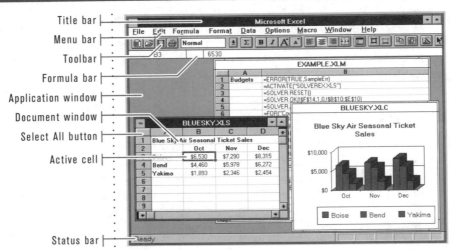

Figure 1-2. *The parts of Excel.*

The *menu bar* shows the command menus available for the active document. In Figure 1-2, the active document is a worksheet; therefore, the menu bar displays the menus for a worksheet. If the active document were a chart, the menu bar would display the menus for a chart.

The *toolbar* is the strip of buttons immediately beneath the menu bar. You can carry out common commands quickly by clicking the appropriate button. By default, Excel displays the Standard toolbar. You can customize this toolbar or open other toolbars—you'll learn how in the next chapter. The sidebar "The Standard toolbar" gives a quick rundown of what each button (on the Standard toolbar) does.

Just below the toolbar is the *formula bar* that displays information about the active cell (Figure 1-3). The *active cell* is a single cell that you've selected by itself or a single cell within a selected group of cells. It has a dark border around it. If you haven't activated the formula bar, the rest of the formula bar is blank. To activate the formula bar, click on it.

The *reference area* shows the active cell's row and column. The contents of the active cell are displayed in the *entry area*.

The entry area has a flashing vertical bar called the *insertion point*, which marks the point where the text you type will appear. The *enter button* stores the data in the formula bar into the cell (pressing Enter on the keyboard does the same thing). The *cancel button* lets you revert to the data that was in the cell when you activated the formula bar (pressing the Esc key does the same thing).

Reference area   Cancel button   Enter button   Entry area

A1

Figure 1-3.

The *status bar* at the bottom of the workspace gives a short description of the current command or Excel's current status.

In the upper left corner of the worksheet window, there is a *Select All button*, which you use to select all the cells in the worksheet.

Now you know the lay of the land. For those of you who can't wait to get your hands on all of Excel's features, the sidebar "If you're really, *really* in a hurry" gives you the basics.

STAYING ON FRIENDLY TERMS WITH EXCEL

Working with Excel can be like serving as a diplomat to a foreign country. You need to learn a few new customs before you can feel comfortable. To avoid the frustration of spreadsheet culture shock, follow these rules:

1. *Put detail information at the top left.* Excel calculates top to bottom, left to right. You'll speed up calculations by going with Excel's flow—especially in worksheets with complex formulas.

2. *Put summaries and totals at the bottom right.*

3. *Put long categories in rows.* Excel has 16,384 rows but only 256 columns. In addition, Excel can show more rows on the screen than columns.

4. *Name the parts of your worksheet.* Naming the parts of your worksheet helps you find them fast and

1

The Standard toolbar

Here's what you get with Excel's Standard toolbar:

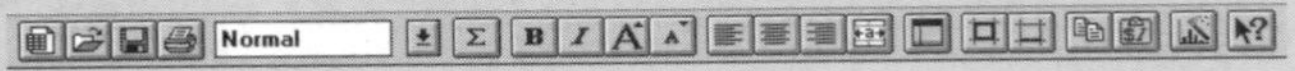

Figure 1-4. *The Standard toolbar*

New Worksheet tool creates a new worksheet.

Open File tool opens a document.

Save File tool saves the active document.

Print tool prints the active document.

Normal **Style box** records cell formats and applies them to other cells.

AutoSum tool sums the values in a range of cells.

Bold and **Italic tools** make text bold or italic.

Increase Font Size tool increases the font size.

Decrease Font Size tool decreases font size.

ensures the accuracy of your formulas. (In Chapter 2, I'll explain how.)

5. *Use a staggered layout to avoid accidentally deleting material.* If you have a worksheet with several separate sections, start at the upper left corner and

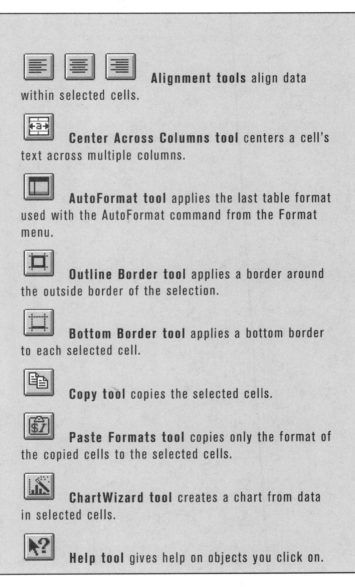

Alignment tools align data within selected cells.

Center Across Columns tool centers a cell's text across multiple columns.

AutoFormat tool applies the last table format used with the AutoFormat command from the Format menu.

Outline Border tool applies a border around the outside border of the selection.

Bottom Border tool applies a bottom border to each selected cell.

Copy tool copies the selected cells.

Paste Formats tool copies only the format of the copied cells to the selected cells.

ChartWizard tool creates a chart from data in selected cells.

Help tool gives help on objects you click on.

position the sections diagonally (Figure 1-5). This also leaves room to expand an area.

1

If you're really, *really* in a hurry

You've got a presentation due in two hours? You've got to get some work done *now*? Here are some frequently used features. I'll give you a quick explanation of each, but you have to promise to come back and read the rest of the book. Promise?

- *Entering text and numbers.* Select the cell. Type the text or value. Press Enter. That's it!

- *Entering a formula.* Select the cell where you want the formula. Type an equals sign (=). Then type the formula. For example, =A1+B1. Press Enter.

- *Summing a range of cells.* Put the cursor in the cell where you want the sum. Click the AutoSum button (the one with the Σ on it), select the range of cells you want to sum, and press Enter.

- *Formatting cells.* Select the cells you want to format. Click the selection with the right mouse button. A shortcut menu appears. From the menu, select the format you want for the selection. For example, you can change font settings (font, size, color, and type style) by choosing Font and selecting settings from the Font dialog box.

- *Formatting cells FAST.* You can apply formats fast with toolbars. For example, make text bold by selecting cells and clicking the **B** button (Bold tool) in the Standard toolbar. Or pick a tool from the Formatting toolbar (enabled with the Toolbars command from the Options menu).

- *Formatting cells REALLY FAST.* If you don't have the time to fiddle with formats, you can apply one of Excel's predefined table formats. Select the cells to format, choose AutoFormat from the Format menu, select the format from the Table Format list box (you'll see a sample of the format in the Sample box), and click OK.

1

- *Changing how numbers, times, and dates are displayed.* Select the cells. Click the selection with the right mouse button. A shortcut menu appears. From the menu, select Number. In the Number Format dialog box, select the number style you want to use and click OK.

- *Moving cells.* Select the cells, with the left mouse button select the outer border of the cells, drag to a new location, and release the mouse button.

- *Copying cells.* Select the cells, hold down the Ctrl key, use the left mouse button to select the outside border of the cells, drag the cells to where you want to copy them, and release the button.

- *Entering a series of numbers, dates, or times.* Type the starting value in the cell where you want to begin the series. Type the second value in the next cell. Select both cells and use the left mouse button to drag the fill handle (the small box at the bottom right corner of the selection) until you've expanded the selection into the series you want.

- *Creating and editing charts.* Select the cells that contain the chart values. Click the ChartWizard button on the toolbar (the one with a bar chart and magic wand). Draw a box anywhere on the worksheet. The ChartWizard guides you through five steps for creating a chart. Make the settings in each dialog box and click the Next button to accept them and move on to the next step. For the details on handling charts, see Chapter 5.

- *Printing.* To print the active document on your default Windows printer, choose Print from the File menu. To preview the printed page(s) before you actually print the document on paper, choose Print Preview from the File menu.

1

Groups of cells
diagonally positioned

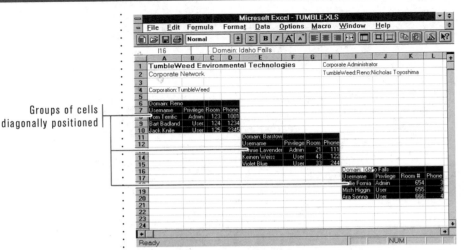

Figure 1-5. *Use a diagonal design to avoid accidentally deleting cells that are underneath or to the side of the section you're working on.*

N ow that you've learned your way around, it's time to pick up some essential Excel skills—skills that you'll use every time you work with Excel.

CHAPTER 2

LEARNING THE ESSENTIALS

So far I've just shown you around. Now I'm going to teach you two key skills you need to get your work done.

Working with Excel is as simple as selecting cells and then carrying out an action. You do everything this way, even complex commands (such as the database features or the Goal Seek function).

But first things first. You can't select cells if you can't get to them. In this chapter, you'll learn three important skills:

- How to select cells

- How to navigate within a worksheet

- How to carry out commands quickly, using shortcut menus and toolbars

SELECTING CELLS

The smallest unit of selection is a single cell. To select a cell, click on it with the mouse or move to it with the arrow keys. When you select a single cell, you make that cell *active*. The active cell has a darkened border (Figure 2-1). When a cell is active, it's ready for you to enter a value or formula into it. Its cell reference also appears in the cell reference box.

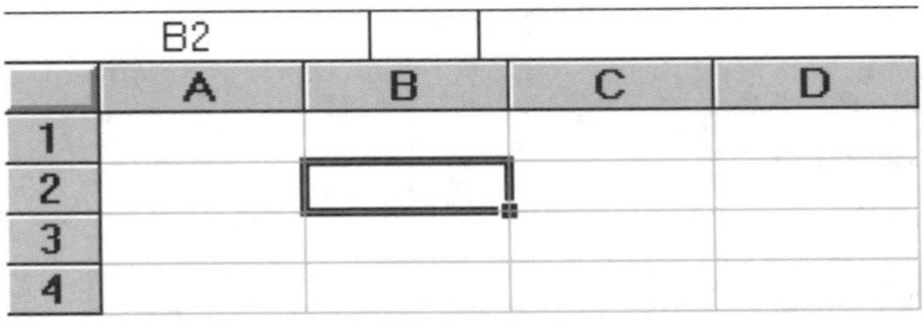

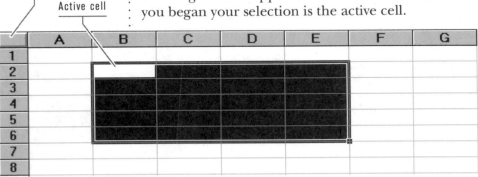

Figure 2-1. *The active cell has a darkened border.*

Selecting groups of cells

Suppose you want to make the entries in a group of cells bold. It would be tedious to change them one at a time. Don't worry. In Excel, you can select multiple cells (called *ranges*) and work on them simultaneously (Figure 2-2).

To select a range of cells, drag from one corner of the range to the opposite corner. The corner where you began your selection is the active cell.

Select All button

Active cell

Figure 2-2. *Selected cells are highlighted.*

When you select a group of cells, a dark border appears around the outside of the selection and the cells in the selection have a dark background. The active cell within the selection has a light background.

> ### *Extending a selection.*
> What if you want to extend the selection? Simple. Hold down the Shift key and click on the selected cells. Then, without releasing the mouse button, drag until you've extended the selection. When the selection is the size you want, release the mouse button. You can also use the same technique to make a selection smaller.

You'll find that you need to select some special groups of cells again and again, such as all the cells in a row or a column. Or you'll need to select cells that aren't grouped together in one rectangular block. Here's how to handle those special selections:

- **Selecting all cells in the worksheet.** To select every cell in the worksheet, click the Select All button (Figure 2-2).

- **Selecting rows and columns**. Selecting an entire row or column is easy—just click its heading.

- **Selecting noncontinuous ranges of cells.** Sometimes you need to select ranges that are not side by side. Here's how to do it: Select the first range. Then hold down the Ctrl key, click where you want to begin the next range, and drag until that range is selected (Figure 2-3). You can also continue to add more ranges this way.

	A	B	C	D	E	F	G
1	███	███					
2	███	███		███	███		
3				███	███		
4				███	███		
5		███		███	███		
6	███	███					
7							
8							

Figure 2-3. *Use the Ctrl key and the mouse to select noncontinuous groups of cells.*

MOVING
WITHIN A
WORKSHEET

Usually Excel can show only part of your worksheet at one time because most worksheets have more data than the screen can display. (See the sidebar "Zooming for a better view" to find out how to zoom to see more of your worksheet.) Therefore, you need to know how to move big distances (more than one cell at a time) within the worksheet.

You can move around one cell at a time using the arrow keys. But you can move greater distances in a single bound by using the scroll bars, which work exactly the way they do in all other Windows programs (Figure 2-4). You can use the scroll bar at the bottom of the document window to move across (left and right) the worksheet. The scroll bar at right side of the document window lets you move up and down the worksheet.

Scroll arrows move one row or column at a time

Scroll boxes move to a relative position

Shaded area moves one screen at a time

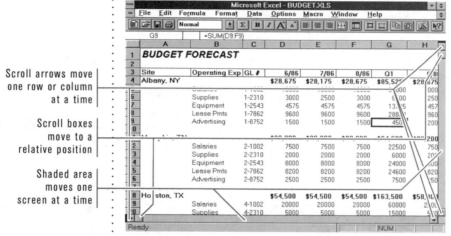

Figure 2-4. *Use scroll bars to move around a worksheet.*

Moving fast by naming cells

When you work with a big spreadsheet, you need a better way to move around. The best method is to name the sections. Then you can jump to each section with a single command. Here's how it works:

First, you name the range of cells. Select the range and choose Define Name from the Formula menu. The

Define Name dialog box appears (Figure 2-5). Excel puts the text in the active cell in the Name text box. You can use the name Excel suggests or type a different name. To define the name, click OK (or click Add).

From now on you can move to this range by using the Goto command from the Formula menu.

To go to a named range, choose Goto from the Formula menu, select the name of the range from the Goto list box, and click OK.

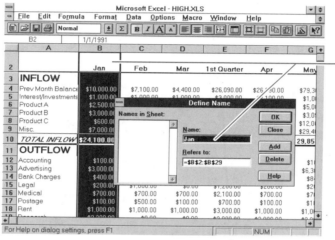

Contents of active cell are suggested as a name

Figure 2-5. *Name groups of cells for easy reference and fast selection.*

Note that Excel doesn't distinguish between upper-case and lowercase letters when it deals with names.

To remove a name from a range, choose Define Name from the Formula menu. Select the name of the range from the Names In Sheet list box, and click Delete. When you finish deleting names, click OK.

H alf the battle of learning Excel is finding the right command or tool to do what you want. Once you find the right tool, it's usually pretty simple to use.

Everytime you select anything (cells, graphic objects, charts, or the elements of a chart), you're one mouse click from the most common commands for that selection.

FINDING THE TOOLS YOU WANT

2

Zooming for a better view

Wish you could see more cells of a big worksheet or get a close-up of just a few cells? With Excel, you can magnify or reduce the size in which the worksheet appears—without affecting the actual size of cells or objects on the worksheet.

To zoom to a magnified or reduced view, choose Zoom from the Window menu. From the Magnification buttons, select the magnification at which you want to view the worksheet. Click OK (Figure 2-6).

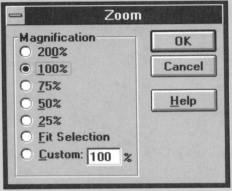

Figure 2-6. *Choose how much to reduce or enlarge using the Magnification buttons.*

If you select 200%, you double the viewed size of the original (get a close up). If you select 25%, you reduce the viewed size to 25% (zoom out for the "big picture").

You can also specify any zoom percentage between 10% and 400% by selecting Custom and typing the amount in the % entry box. The Fit Selection button magnifies the worksheet so that the currently selected cells fit completely in the document window (if possible).

For a sample of zoomed views, take a look at Figures 2-7 and 2-8.

2

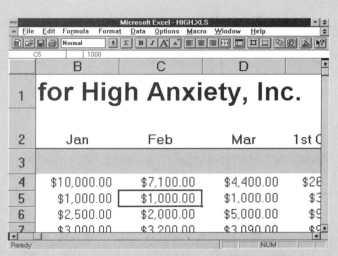

Figure 2-7. *The example HIGH.XLS worksheet at 200% magnification.*

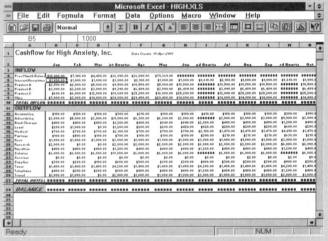

Figure 2-8. *The HIGH.XLS worksheet at 50% magnification.*

Later in this chapter, you'll learn how to add zoom buttons to the toolbar so you can zoom the views by clicking a button.

2

Excel gives you many ways to carry out actions. The two handiest ones are shortcut menus and toolbars.

Using shortcut menus

Shortcut menus put the most common commands for the selection in a single menu. Just select what you want to work on and click the right mouse button. A shortcut menu appears. From the shortcut menu, choose what you want to do with the selection.

For example, you can apply a number format to cells containing numbers by selecting the cells, clicking the selection with the right mouse button, choosing Number from the shortcut menu (Figure 2-9), selecting the number format from the dialog box, and clicking OK.

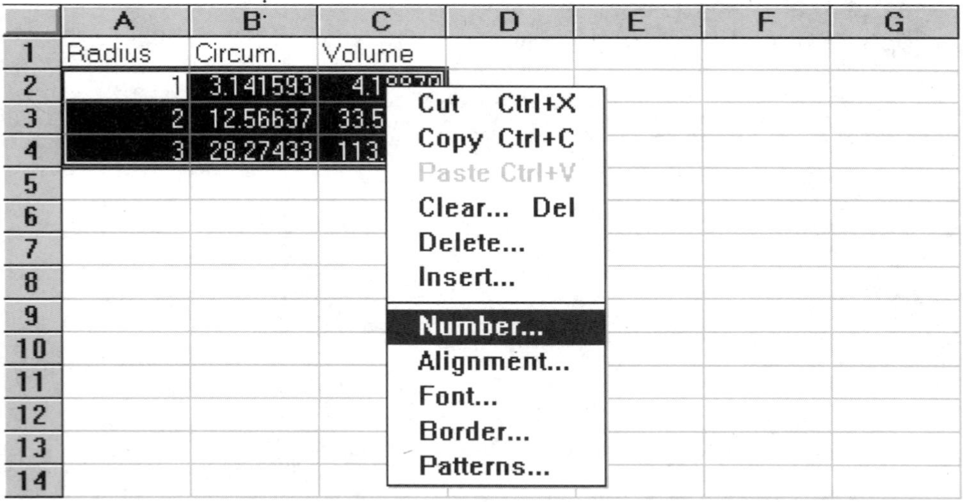

	A	B	C	D	E	F	G
1	Radius	Circum.	Volume				
2	1	3.141593	4.18879				
3	2	12.56637	33.5				
4	3	28.27433	113.				
5							
6							
7							
8							
9							
10							
11							
12							
13							
14							

Cut Ctrl+X
Copy Ctrl+C
Paste Ctrl+V
Clear... Del
Delete...
Insert...
Number...
Alignment...
Font...
Border...
Patterns...

Figure 2-9. *Select what you want to work on and click on it with the right mouse button.*

Using toolbars

Toolbars let you carry out a command by just clicking a button. By default, Excel displays its Standard toolbar just below the menu bar.

To carry out a command using the toolbar, select the cells, graphic objects, or chart elements. Then

18

click the appropriate button in the toolbar. For example, you can sum a group of cells by selecting the cell that will contain the total, clicking the Σ (Auto-Sum) button, and selecting the cells you want to sum.

> ### *Deciphering Toolbar hieroglyphics*
> If you can't decipher the symbols on the toolbar buttons, click the toolbar button with the left mouse button and hold it down. A short description of the command appears in the status bar at the bottom of the screen. If you don't want to execute the command, continue holding down the mouse button, move the cursor off the button, and release the mouse button.

If you can't find the commands you need on the Standard toolbar, choose Toolbars from the Options menu. The Toolbars dialog box appears (Figure 2-10). From the Show Toolbars list box, select the toolbar that suits your needs. The new toolbar will appear as a "floating" window with buttons (Figure 2-11). It will stay in place—even if you scroll or resize the worksheet that's underneath. You can put the new toolbar underneath (or above) the Standard toolbar by dragging the toolbar window (a dotted outline gives a preview of where it will go).

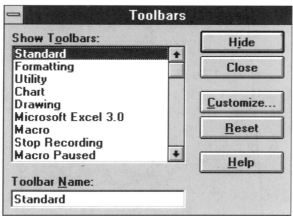

Figure 2-10. *From the Show Toolbars list box, select the toolbars you want to use.*

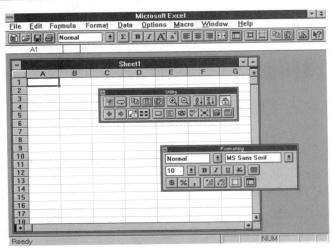

Figure 2-11. *Toolbars you've added appear in their own floating windows on the workspace.*

> ### Shortcut for adding more toolbars
> If there are already toolbars in the workspace, you can use the right mouse button to click on any of the toolbars to make a shortcut menu appear. You can choose the toolbar you want from the shortcut menu.

To make a toolbar disappear, double-click on the toolbar window's control button.

Creating a custom toolbar

Excel's regular toolbars have many of the most common commands—but that doesn't mean that they're the ones you want. So why not make your own toolbar with just the right buttons? It's easy.

To create a custom toolbar, choose Toolbars from the Options menu (or click a toolbar with the right mouse button and choose Toolbars from the shortcut menu). In the Toolbar Name text box, type a name for the custom toolbar. Then click Add (Figure 2-12). A floating toolbar appears with the custom name but with no buttons on it. The Customize dialog box also appears (Figure 2-13). Select the category of the but-

2

ton you want from the Categories list box. The buttons for that category will then appear in the Tools box. Add the buttons you want by dragging them from the Tools box to the toolbar you just created. When you're done, click Close.

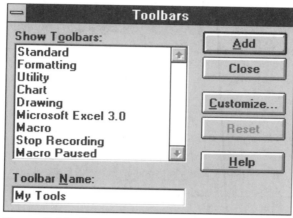

Figure 2-12. *To create a new toolbar, type the name for your new toolbar in the Toolbar Name text box and click Add.*

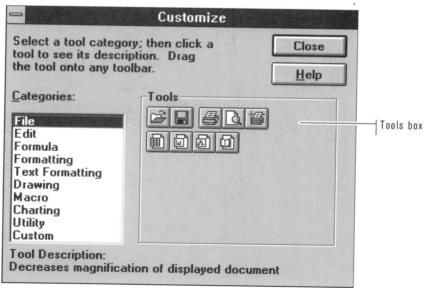

Figure 2-13. *Drag the tools you need from the Tools box.*

To take tools off a toolbar, make sure the toolbar is enabled, click on it with the right mouse button,

Toolbar tips

Throughout the rest of the book, I'll give you tips on handy buttons to add to your custom toolbar. Try adding some now by creating a custom toolbar and adding the two zoom tools (Zoom In and Zoom Out) from the Utilities category (Figure 2-0). These two tools will let you zoom the view of the worksheet (see the sidebar "Zooming for a better view" earlier in this chapter).

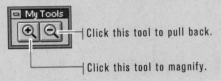

Click this tool to pull back.

Click this tool to magnify.

choose Customize from the shortcut menu, drag the tool off the toolbar, and click Close.

Now you've got your own toolbar with just the commands you want. You can display it or hide it just like any of Excel's regular toolbars.

That wasn't so hard, was it? You've already learned your way around, picked up two essential skills, and found out how to quickly find the commands you want. In the next chapter, I'll show you a quick, simple way to set up a worksheet.

CHAPTER 3

SETTING UP A WORKSHEET

Building a worksheet may seem intimidating if you're new to spreadsheets. But suppose I told you that you can build any worksheet with just three steps:

1. Enter the text.

2. Enter the numbers.

3. Enter the formulas.

Usually, you use text for row and column titles, numbers to store your raw data, and formulas for your analysis of the data.

ake a look at Figure 3-1. The text consists of phrases such as "Cash Flow for High Anxiety, Inc" and "Inflow" and names of months. The numbers are values such as the $100 accounting expense in cell B12.

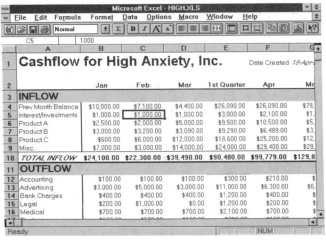

Figure 3-1. *A worksheet has at least three parts.*

As for the formulas, they're invisible in this picture, but their results are plain to see. The $24,100 shown in cell B10, for instance, is the result of a formula that tells Excel, "Sum the numbers in cells B4 through B9, and display the result."

There are only three steps to build any worksheet, no matter how complex. Oh sure, you can take additional steps to touch it up. You can edit and format it (as I'll show you in Chapter 4) or add a chart (Chapter 5) or print it out (Chapter 6).

But those things are the frosting. At the core, every single Excel worksheet consists of three parts. Follow along as I show you how to enter text, numbers, and formulas to build an Excel worksheet.

ENTERING TEXT

hether you're dealing with text or numbers, you enter them with three simple steps: (1) select the cell, (2) type the value, and (3) press Enter (Figures 3-2 through 3-4). (You select a cell by clicking on it with the mouse, or by navigating to it with the arrow keys. But you knew that already.)

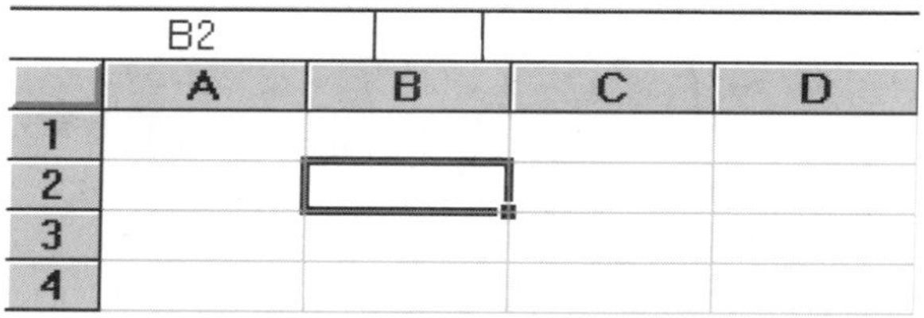

Figure 3-2. *Select the cell,...*

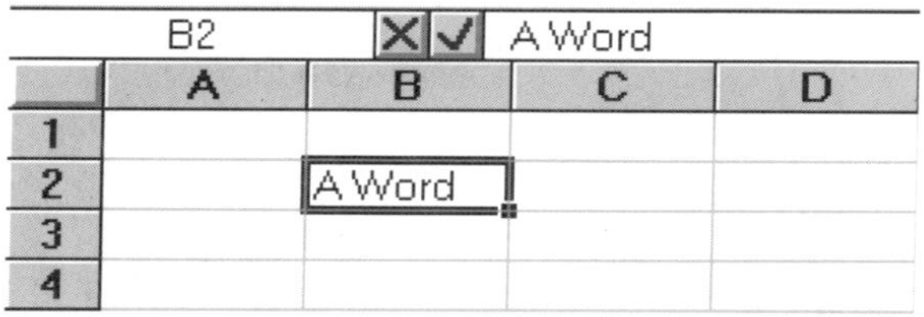

Figure 3-3. *...Type the value,...*

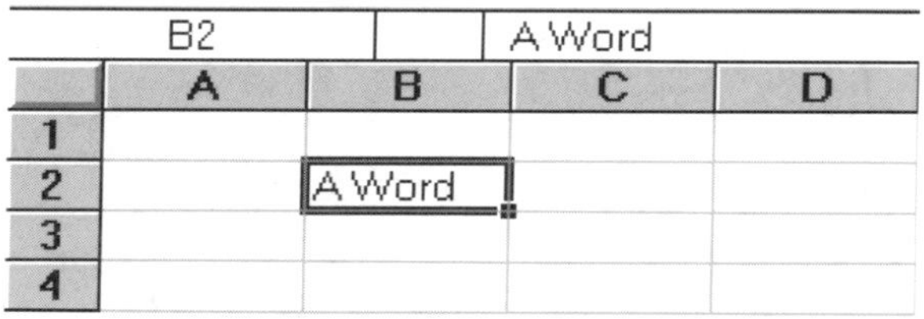

Figure 3-4. *...And press the Enter key to store the value inside the cell.*

Formulas work a little differently, as you'll see.

Excel stores all the text you type, even if it can't fit inside the cell (up to 255 characters, that is). The characters appear both in the cell and in the formula bar (Figure 3-6). The actual contents of the cell appear in the formula bar; however, all the characters that you type may not be able to fit in the cell. So Excel scrolls the text through the cell as you type—the way stock reports move across a marquee at the New York Stock Exchange.

3

Setting up files

Ready to get started? Not so fast! You don't want your hard work to disappear, do you? The first thing you should do—the **first** thing—when you start a worksheet is to save the file. Once you've saved the file for the first time, you can record your progress by choosing Save from the File menu (or by pressing the keyboard shortcut Alt-F-S). I recommend pressing Alt-F-S every five minutes, or whenever you pause for more than a few seconds. It's just safer that way.

When you first start Excel, a document window called Sheet1 appears in the workspace. This is a new worksheet ready for you to use. (You can also create a new worksheet at any time by choosing New from the File menu, selecting Worksheet, and clicking OK.)

You save the worksheet by choosing Save from the File menu (Figure 3-5).

Figure 3-5. *Use File Save to save the worksheet as a file.*

Excel automatically enters a name in the File Name text box (SHEET1.XLS, for example). Delete the generic name and give the worksheet a more descriptive filename (CASHFLOW.XLS, for instance). Simply type the filename in the text box. You can leave off the extension (.XLS), and Excel automatically adds it for you. Then use the Directories list box to navigate to the directory where you want the file. Click OK to save the file.

But what if you're not starting from scratch? What if you want to reopen a worksheet from a previous session? To open an existing worksheet, choose Open from the File menu. Use the Directories list box to navigate to the directory where the worksheet file is, and double-click on the worksheet's filename in the File Name list box. The worksheet appears in the workspace.

Creating a backup file for a worksheet

You can tell Excel to store the previous version of an individual worksheet file. To do this, choose Save As from the File menu, click Options, and enable the Create Backup File check box. Then click OK twice to accept your options and save the file. A message box that says "Replacing Existing *filename*" may appear (where *filename* is the filename of the worksheet). This means that Excel is replacing the old version of the worksheet and its option settings (before you added the backup option) with the current version of your worksheet that has the backup option. Be sure that the filename and path are the correct and click OK. Now each time you save the file, Excel stores the previous version as a backup. The backup file is in the same directory as the worksheet and has the same name but with the BAK extension.

3

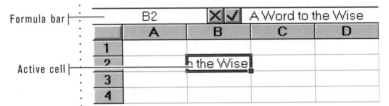

Formula bar

Active cell

Figure 3-6. *When you enter text, the stored value appears in the formula bar. If you type more text than can fit, the text scrolls through the cell as you type.*

After you press Enter to store a long entry, the text expands over the next few cells so that all the text is displayed—provided the adjacent cells are empty (Figure 3-7). If those cells contain data, Excel shows as much text as it can fit within the cell (Figure 3-8).

	A	B	C	D
1				
2		A Word to the Wise		
3				
4				

B2   A Word to the Wise

Figure 3-7. *Text that won't fit in one cell fills the cells to the right if those cells are empty.*

	A	B	C	D
1				
2		A Word to	123	456
3				
4				

B2   A Word to the Wise

Figure 3-8. *If the adjacent cells contain text, Excel shows as much as it can—but the text appears chopped off.*

> ### Inserting line breaks
> Sometimes, you'll have a long title for a column and you'll want the text to wrap (go to the next line) after a specific word. You can do this by inserting a line break after that word. First, you need to make sure Wrap Text is enabled for the cell in which you're entering text (choose Alignment from the Format menu, enable the Wrap Text check box, and click OK). To insert a line break, type Alt-Enter.

Fitting text into cells

If all the text won't fit, you can make the cell bigger, or you can turn on word wrap.

To widen the column, place the mouse cursor between the headings of the cells. The cursor turns into a double-ended arrow. Now drag the column border until the cell is wide enough to hold the text. If you don't want to widen the column, you can make the row taller. The process is the same. You drag the row border to expand the cell.

B2		A Word to the Wise	
	A	B	C
1			
2		A Word to the Wise	
3			
4			

Figure 3-9. *The cell from Figure 3-7 with column B resized to hold all the text in cell B2.*

There's another way to make text fit into a cell. If word wrap is on, Excel automatically expands the cell height until all the characters appear. Simply select the cell, click the cell with the right mouse button, choose Alignment from the shortcut menu (Figure 3-11), select Wrap Text, and click OK (Figure 3-10).

3

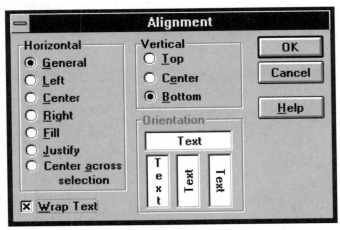

Figure 3-11. *Enable the Wrap Text check box to turn on word wrap.*

Double-click here to widen column B's width.

Double-click here to increase the row 2's height.

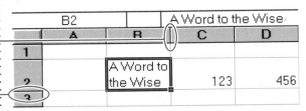

Figure 3-10. *Column B has the standard width—but the Wrap Text option expands the height of the row so that all the text appears.*

Shortcut for resizing columns and rows

Want the column to be just wide enough to fit the text? Double-click on the border between the column headings. Want the row to be tall enough to fit the words? Double-click on the border between the row headings. In the example, you could use this technique to either expand the column width or row height of cell B2 (Figure 3-10). Excel will figure out just how big to make it, and do the work for you.

Creating row and column titles

When you have more rows and columns than you can fit on one screen, Excel gives you a way to continue to see the titles you've given each row and column as you scroll through your worksheet. Excel lets you keep your row and column titles frozen on the screen as you scroll through the rest of the worksheet. For example, the worksheet that stores the art information for this book has the first two rows frozen so I can still see the column titles when I scroll down the rows—note that I've scrolled down to row 22 (Figure 3-12).

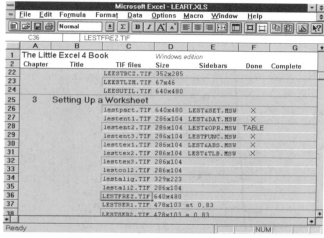

Figure 3-12. *This worksheet has the first two rows frozen so that the column titles are always in view.*

To freeze the column titles (this works the same way for row titles), select the row beneath the column titles (usually this is your first row of data), choose Freeze Panes from the Window menu.

To unfreeze the column titles, choose Unfreeze Panes from the Window menu.

To freeze both row and column titles...

...select the first cell of data. Instead of freezing the row and column titles individually, you can select the cell just to the right of the row titles and just below the column titles to do both. Excel splits the display of the worksheet above or to the left of the selection. If the selection is a single cell, the top and left of the cell is used to split the worksheet.

3

ENTERING NUMBERS

So far we've been talking about text, but most of the data you enter will be numbers: currency, percentages, real numbers, fractions, and dates. To work with numbers, you need to know how to tell Excel what kind of number you want. Here's how it works:

- **To enter a positive number** without any other formatting, select the cell, type the number, and press Enter.

- **To enter negative numbers**, precede the number with a minus sign (-) or enclose it in parentheses. For example, enter negative twelve by typing -12 or (12).

- **To enter currency numbers** (U.S. dollars), precede the value with a dollar sign ($). For example, enter 5 dollars and 35 cents by typing $5.35.

- **To enter percentages**, follow the value with a percent sign (%). For example, enter 25 percent by typing 25%.

- **To enter fractions**, separate the numerator and denominator with a slash (/). All fractions must be preceded by a divisor (a whole number) and a space; otherwise, Excel will store the value as a date. For example, enter three-and-one-half by typing 3 1/2 (don't forget the space after the 3). Fractions such as ½ must be preceded by a zero. For example, you would enter one-half by typing 0 1/2.

- **To enter numbers in scientific (or exponential) notation**, type the value in the cell and choose Number from the Format menu. Select the 0.00E+00 number format, and click OK. Excel displays all exponential numbers in this format: the number, followed by an E (which stands for exponent), followed by a plus or minus sign and the value of the exponent. For example, if you type the number 22668, Excel displays it as 2.27E+04 (2.27 times ten to the fourth power). Excel automatically displays numbers in exponential format if the number of digits exceeds the cell space.

- **To enter dates**, you can use any of several formats. You can spell out the date (April 21, 1992; Apr 21, 1992), or you can type it with numbers and hyphens (21-apr-92), or numbers and slashes (4/21/92). Excel tries to match your entry with one of its built-in date formats. If it can't recognize your entry (if you misspelled the month, for example), it stores it as text. For information on how Excel handles dates, see the sidebar "How Excel stores dates and times."

- **To enter times**, you separate hours, minutes, and seconds with colons (:). Excel recognizes a 12-hour clock or a 24-hour clock (international time). By default, Excel uses the 24-hour clock. To enter times with the 24-hour clock, simply type the time. For example, 3:15 in the afternoon is entered as 15:15. To use the 12-hour clock, follow the time with a space and the letters AM or PM. For example, 3:15 in the afternoon is entered as 3:15 PM.

When you type a number as I've just shown you, Excel chooses a format in which to display it. In Chapter 4, I'll explain how to switch to a different format if you don't like the one Excel has chosen.

Entering a series

You often need to enter a series of dates or numbers. For instance, the date series January, February, March, etc. appears in many, many worksheets.

Why enter these values one at a time when Excel can do it for you? It's simple. Enter the first two values into the two cells that will be at the beginning of your series. Then select the two cells and drag the selection's fill handle until you've expanded the series into all the cells you want (Figures 3-14 and 3-15).

3

How Excel stores dates & times

As far as Excel is concerned, dates and times are simply special types of numbers. In fact, they are stored as decimal values, not as the characters you typed.

When you enter the date April 21, 1992, it is displayed in the formula bar as 4/21/1992. But that's not the value Excel stores. Excel has a range of dates from January 1, 1900 to December 31, 2078, which are assigned a number from 1 to 65,380. It uses these numbers to record the date.

Times are also assigned special numbers: 0.0 to 0.999 for 12:00 A.M. to 11:59:59 P.M. You might think this is a little weird, but this method of recording dates lets you make time and date calculations, such as counting the number of days between two dates (Figure 3-13).

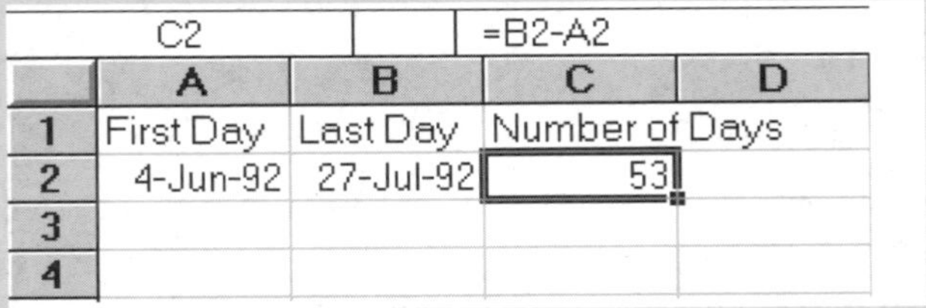

C2		=B2-A2	
	A	**B**	**C**	**D**
1	First Day	Last Day	Number of Days	
2	4-Jun-92	27-Jul-92	53	
3				
4				

Figure 3-13. *Excel lets you make date and time calculations—such as finding the number of days within a time period.*

If you accidently apply a decimal number format to a date, the stored decimal value will appear in the cell. To return the displayed value to a date, select the cell, click on it with the right mouse button, choose Number from the shortcut menu, select Date from the Category list box, select a date format from the Format Codes list box, and click OK.

3

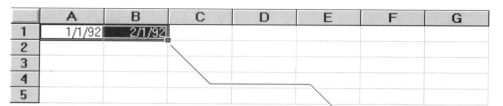

Figure 3-14. *Type the first two values and select them...*   Fill handle

	A	B	C	D	E	F	G
1	1/1/92	2/1/92	3/1/92	4/1/92	5/1/92	6/1/92	
2							
3							
4							
5							

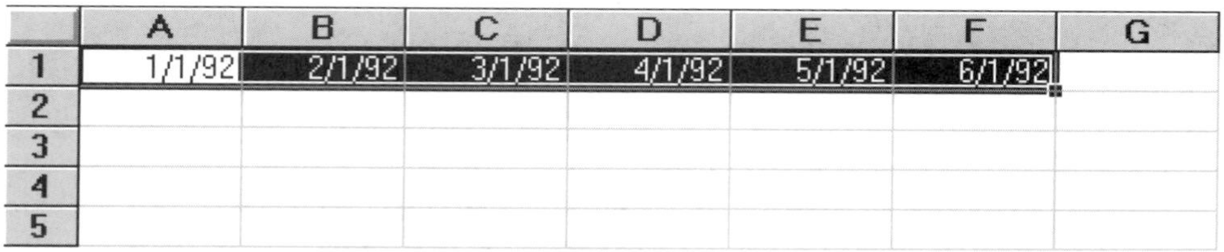

Figure 3-15. *...Then drag the fill handle to extend the series.*

Excel uses the difference (called the *step value*) between the first two values you entered to generate the series. For example, if you enter 3/1/92 and 4/1/92, Excel expands the series into dates that increase by one month (3/1/92, 4/1/92, 5/1/92, 6/1/92, and so on).

This method works well for most series; however, some series are more complex. For example, suppose you want to increment a number by multiplying it (multiples of two: 2, 4, 8, 16, and so on).

For complex series, use this method: Select the cells to contain the series. Be sure the first cell contains the correct starting value. Now use Series from the Data menu to specify the type of series (number or date), the step value, and the stop value (Figure 3-16).

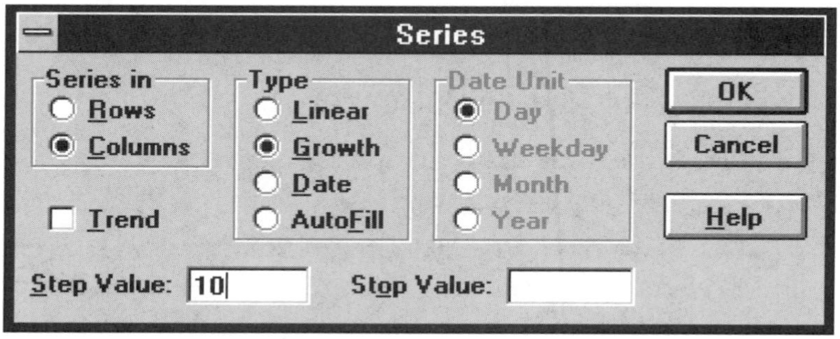

Series

Series in
- ○ **R**ows
- ● **C**olumns

□ **T**rend

Type
- ○ **L**inear
- ● **G**rowth
- ○ **D**ate
- ○ Auto**F**ill

Date Unit
- ● **D**ay
- ○ **W**eekday
- ○ **M**onth
- ○ **Y**ear

OK

Cancel

Help

Step Value: 10   S**t**op Value: [ ]

Figure 3-16. *You can specify how Excel generates a date or number series.*

Excel uses the step value to increment the series. By default, Excel generates series by adding one to the number value or date unit as it moves across a row (or down a column). (A *date unit* is one part of a date: the day, day of week, month, or year.) If you have two numbers or two dates in the first two cells, Excel displays settings (such as step value) that represent the difference between those two values. Of course, you can change these settings.

When you generate a series of numbers, you can choose whether to add or multiply by the step value. A *linear series* increases by adding the step value each time. (Use a negative number if you want the series to decrease.) For instance, you might use a linear series to show a projection that target sales will increase by 10 units each month (Figure 3-17).

Excel generates a *growth series* by multiplying by the step value each time. For instance, you might use a growth series to see what would happen if sales increased by 10% each month (wouldn't that be nice!).

Linear series

Growth series

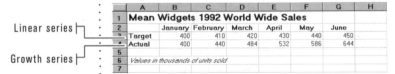

	A	B	C	D	E	F	G	H
1	Mean Widgets 1992 World Wide Sales							
2		January	February	March	April	May	June	
3	Target	400	410	420	430	440	450	
4	Actual	400	440	484	532	586	644	
5								
6	Values in thousands of units sold							
7								

Figure 3-17. *Two ways to generate a series of numbers.*

Excel keeps generating the series until it reaches the end of the selected cells in the row (or column) *unless* you specify a *stop value* in the Series dialog box. If you specify a stop value, Excel stops when it reaches that value.

Entering text and numbers fast

Here are some tips that will save you extra typing when entering text and numbers:

■ **Using fixed decimal entry.** Often you enter numbers that have the same number of decimal places (dollars and cents, for example). You can set up Excel so that it knows where to put the decimal point—you don't even need to type it. Choose Workspace from the Options menu. Enable the Fixed Decimal check box. In the Places entry box, type the number of decimal places you want. Click OK. Now all you have to do is enter the number and Excel inserts the decimal place automatically. To disable fixed decimal entry, choose Workspace from the Options menu and disable the Fixed Decimal check box.

- **Moving down to the next cell automatically.** Normally when you press the Enter key, Excel accepts your input and the current cell remains selected. To type something in the next cell, you have to select the cell manually. To save time, tell Excel to move the selection each time you press Enter. Choose Workspace from the Options menu, enable the Move Selection After Enter check box, and click OK. Now Excel will jump down to the next cell as soon as you press Enter.

- **Entering the current date or time.** To enter the current date in a cell, press Ctrl-; (semicolon). To enter the current time, press Ctrl-Shift-: (colon).

- **Copying the formula or value from the cell above.** Here's two shortcuts that copy the formula or value from the cell above active cell to the active cell. To copy the formula, press Ctrl-' (apostrophe). To copy the value, press Ctrl-Shift-" (double quotation mark).

ENTERING FORMULAS

So far, you've learned how to enter text and numbers. But the real power of Excel doesn't come into play until you start entering formulas.

When you enter text and numbers, you're telling Excel to store and display exactly what you type. When you enter a formula, you're telling Excel to do something with the values you type in. You're telling it to *evaluate* the formula you've typed and display the answer inside the cell.

A formula can be as simple as a reference to the contents of another cell or as complex as the calculation of structural load on a floor of a skyscraper.

Typing formulas

You enter a formula just as you would text or numbers—except you always begin a formula with an equals sign (=). In fact, if you enter a number as a formula (such as =4), you'll see the formula (=4) in the formula bar and the constant value (4) in the cell.

You can make calculations with numbers by using *operators*, such as addition (+), subtraction (-), multiplication (*), and division (/), and functions. For a list of operators and order of operation, see Table 3-1.

Table 3-1. *Excel operators*

Operator	Description
( )	Parentheses. Expressions within parentheses are always evaluated first.
:	Range
Space	Intersection
,	Union
–	Negation
%	Percent
^	Exponentiation
* and /	Multiplication and division
+ and –	Addition and subtraction
&	Concatenation
= < > <= >= <>	Comparison

To enter a formula:

1. Select the cell.

2. Type an equals sign.

3. Type the formula.

4. Press Enter.

As you type the formula, it appears in the formula bar above the workspace. As soon as you press Enter, Excel goes to work calculating what you've typed and displays the result in the cell. The formula tells Excel what values, operations, and functions to use to calculate the result in the cell.

For example, if you type =2+2, Excel won't show that formula in the cell. Instead, it will calculate and display the result (it's 4, in case you don't have your calculator handy).

Of course, it wouldn't be very beneficial to use Excel for just adding 2+2. It's much more likely that you'll want to tell it something like: "Take the number you find in cell B1, multiply it by 10%, and display the result in cell C2." To do this, you move the cursor to C2, where you type this formula: =B1*0.1 (Figures 3-18 and 3-19).

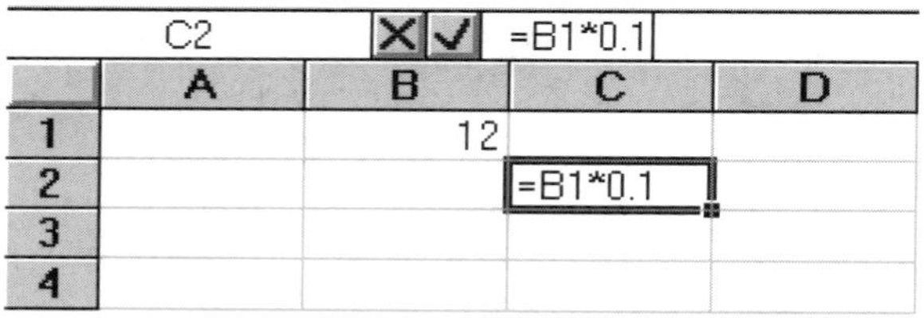

C2	☒ ☑	=B1*0.1	
	A	**B**	**C**	**D**
1		12		
2			=B1*0.1	
3				
4				

Figure 3-18. *Select the cell and type the formula...*

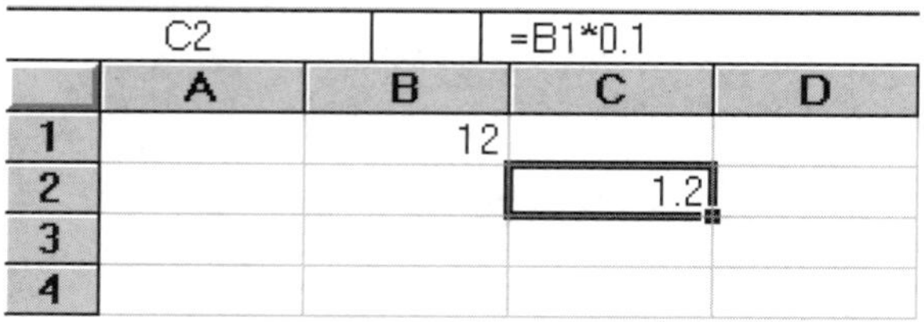

C2		=B1*0.1	
	A	**B**	**C**	**D**
1		12		
2			1.2	
3				
4				

Figure 3-19. *...Then press Enter.*

Using functions

More than likely, your formulas will need to make more advanced calculations than those offered by operators alone (such as addition or multiplication). Excel has a built-in set of functions (such as AVERAGE(), SQRT(), and SIN()) that do most of the calculations required in the real financial, statistical, mathematical, engineering world.

All functions have a name (usually abbreviated, such as SQRT for square root) and are followed by a set of parentheses (SQRT()). Most functions require you to type one or more *arguments* within the parentheses. *Arguments* are the values that Excel uses to evaluate functions. These values can be *constants* (text or numbers), cell references, or even other formulas. For example, the formula =SQRT(4) contains the square root function, has a constant 4 as its argument value, and evaluates to 2.

As another example, you can tell Excel to use the AVERAGE function to: "Add the numbers in cells B3 through B8 and figure the average." That formula would look like this:

    =AVERAGE(B3:B8)

Here's one of the great things about Excel. If you already know which function you need and how it works (what type of arguments it takes, what calculation it makes, and what result it displays), you can just type it in. If not, you can select it from a list with the mouse. To select a function, you choose Paste Function from the Formula menu and pick the one you want from the Paste Function list box (Figure 3-20).

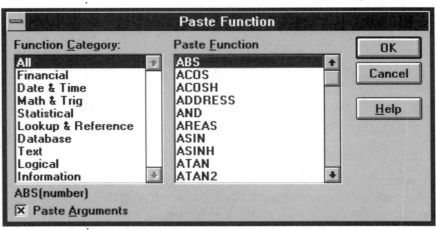

Figure 3-20. *Select the function you want to paste.*

Filtering functions by category
You can display all the functions in the Paste Function list box
(select All from the Function Category list box) or filter them
by category (select the category from Function Category).

Let's say you want to find the maximum value in the range B3 to B8. To enter the function manually, you type:

```
=MAX(B3:B8)
```

To enter this same function from the list, choose Paste Function from the Formula menu. Scroll down the Paste Function list until you see MAX. Select MAX and click OK. Excel inserts it into the formula bar.

If the function requires an argument, enable the Paste Arguments check box and Excel will enter the description of the argument or variable you need to enter into the function. Replace the descriptions with actual values or references. If you check Paste Argument in the example above, the formula bar would look like this:

```
=MAX(number 1, number 2,...)
```

Even if you do not check Paste Argument, you still need to type the argument values into the function.

What kind of functions can you use? Just about anything you can think of. Excel has built-in functions for most advanced mathematical and statistical functions. We don't have space in this book to list them all, but Table 3-2 shows some of the most important functions. If you need the details on a specific function, see the *Microsoft Excel Function Reference* (it's a whole manual devoted solely to Excel functions).

Guidelines for creating formulas

There are seven simple rules to remember as you build formulas:

1.   **Start the formula with an equal sign**. That's the signal telling Excel that this is a formula and not just ordinary text and numbers.

2.   **Remember Excel's order of operations.** As in mathematics, Excel has an order of evaluation that it uses to calculate a formula. This means that Excel always performs operations (^, *, +, and so on) in a specific order. For Excel's order of operation, see Table 3-1. If your formula does not take this order into account, your formula may not give you the results you expect. Excel always evaluates

Table 3-2. *Important Excel functions*

Function	Action	Example	Example result
ABS(value)	Calculates the absolute value of a number.	=ABS(-12)	12
AVERAGE(values)	Calculates the average of values.	=AVERAGE(6,12,2,4)	6
COUNT(values)	Calculates the number of numeric entries in a range.	=COUNT(1,2,4,8,16)	5
IF(condition, true value, false value)	Evaluates an expression to true or false and returns one value for a true condition and another value for a false condition.	=IF(A3>32000, "Bonus", "No Way")	No Way (for A3 equals 27500)
MAX(values)	Finds the maximum value in a range.	=MAX(4,2,5,3,7,1)	7
MIN(values)	Finds the minimum value in a range.	=MIN(4,2,5,3,7,1)	1
MODE(values)	Finds the most common value in a range.	=MODE(3,2,8,2,3,2)	2
NOW()	Calculates the current computer date or time, depending on how the cell is formatted.	=NOW()	12/25/92 (computer date 12/25/92)
PI()	Returns the value of π.	=PI()	3.141592654
PRODUCT(values)	Multiplies values.	=PRODUCT(12,3)	36
ROUND(value, places)	Rounds off a number to a given number of decimal places.	=ROUND(12.886,1)	12.9
SQRT(value)	Calculates the square root.	=SQRT(9)	3
SUM(values)	Adds values.	=SUM(4,2,3,1)	10

3

values within parentheses first. If operators are at the same level of precedence, Excel calculates them left to right.

For example:

```
14+6+20/4=25
```

But:

```
(14+6+20)/4=10
```

3. **Put quotation marks around text in a formula**. For example:

```
=IF(A3>10000, "Bonus", "No
bonus")
```

4. **Separate multiple arguments with a comma.** For example, the Rate function calculates the per-period interest of an annuity. The function requires values for the total number of payment periods, payment amount per period, and the present value. These values are separated in the formula by commas:

```
=RATE(96, -150, 10000)
```

5. **Type relative references with the column letter and the row number**. For example, C5 and J17. For an explanation about how references work, see the sidebar "You absolutely need to learn this."

6. **Type absolute references by preceding the column letters and row numbers with a dollar sign**. For example, $C$5 and $J$17.

7. **Use a colon to refer to a range of cells.** For instance, to include all the cells from B3 to B14, type B3:B14. When using the SUM formula, you can substitute a period for the colon: B3.B14.

Shortcuts for referring to cells

When constructing a formula you can simply type in cell references. But it's usually faster to use one of Excel's two shortcuts:

3

■ **Point to the cells you want.** First, type the formula until you get to a spot that needs a cell reference. Then select cells you want to reference. Excel puts the correct cell reference into the formula bar.

For example, say you want to add cells B3, C4, and D9 and show the result in E10. Start at E10. Type an equal sign to tell Excel you're entering a formula. Click on B3. See how Excel puts the reference in the formula bar for you? Type a plus (+) to tell Excel you want to add another value, and click on C4. Type plus again, and click on D9. Now press Enter.

Even though you didn't type a single cell reference, your formula looks like this:

    =B3+C4+D9

You absolutely need to learn this

You can't use cell references effectively until you learn the difference between *absolute* references and *relative* references. It's not very hard.

An absolute reference is one whose location never changes. No matter how many columns or rows you add or subtract, Excel will always refer back to the original location.

Relative references are much more common and can be more useful. They tell Excel to do something like: "Go to the cell that is two columns over and two rows up and get the value you find there." With a relative reference, you can copy an entire section of your worksheet, and the cell references will still make sense. For instance, if you decide to copy a cell containing a formula with relative references to another cell that's down eight rows, Excel is smart enough to figure out what you've done and adjust the references for you. It will change the cell references so that they point to new locations relative to the copied cell's new position.

3

■ **Name the regions in your worksheet.** Then you can include an entire column, row, or section of cells in a formula just by referring to its name. For more information on naming cells, see Chapter 2.

Relative references only work when...

...you copy cells containing formulas. If you move the cells (using the drag-and-drop technique or using the Cut and Paste commands from the Edit menu), the formulas you move will still refer to the cells that they referred to in the original location.

By default, Excel uses relative references. When you type a cell reference with just its column letter and row number, Excel assumes you want a relative reference. If you want an absolute reference instead, you have to type dollar signs ($) in front of the letter and number. For example:

C5 is a relative reference.
$C$5 is an absolute reference.

To convert a cell reference from one type to the other...

...select the cell with the formula, select the cell reference in the formula bar, and press the F4 key.

Converting cell references to names

When typing a formula, it's usually easier to select the cells you're referencing. But names are easier to remember than cell references. If you've already named the cells you're referring to in your formulas, you can easily convert the cell references into their defined names. Here's how: Select the cells containing the formulas whose references you want to convert, choose Apply Names from the Formula menu, select all the names in the Apply Names list box (or just select the ones you know your formulas refer to), and click OK. Note that Excel can only convert references that have names already defined for them. If the "No References Found" message appears, it means that of your references have no defined names or have already been converted to names.

Now that you know the basic ingredients of worksheets, I'm going to teach you how to customize them to suit your tastes.

Toolbar tip

You already know how the Paste Function dialog box works. By adding the Paste Function tool to your toolbar, you can call it up to paste a function by just clicking the tool.

=ƒ(x)   The **Paste Function tool** lets you select a function and paste it into a cell or formula.

Editing and Formatting a Worksheet

Every building starts with the same basic materials—wood, nails, pipes, beams, and so on. But an architect takes these raw materials and creates something functional and unique. Now that you've got the raw materials for building an Excel worksheet, I'll show you how to customize it to fit your needs.

In this chapter, you'll pick up the skills to fine-tune your worksheet:

- Edit the values and formulas inside cells.

- Move, copy, and delete cell contents.

- Delete and insert cells.

- Format the numbers, alignment, text rotation, font, border, pattern, width, and height of cells.

- Find and replace values or formulas.

- Spellcheck the worksheet.

- Format quickly by using AutoFormat, styles, and templates.

EDITING CELL CONTENTS

xcel makes it easy to change your mind. You can change the contents of cells in two ways: edit the contents or move the cells.

Editing a cell's contents affects only that cell and the cells that have references to it. However, changing the positions of cells by deleting, inserting, and moving them affects the whole worksheet. For example, when you delete a cell, the cells below or to the right are shifted over to fill the vacated space. This may affect cell references and might force cells to intrude into other ranges of cells.

Editing a cell entry is just like using a word processor. First, select the cell and move the mouse cursor to the formula bar (or press F2). Then move the cursor and type the changes. When you finish making changes, press Enter or click on the Enter button (the button with the green check mark). If you don't like your changes, you can revert to the previous cell contents by pressing Esc or clicking on the Cancel button (the button with the red X) (Figure 4-1).

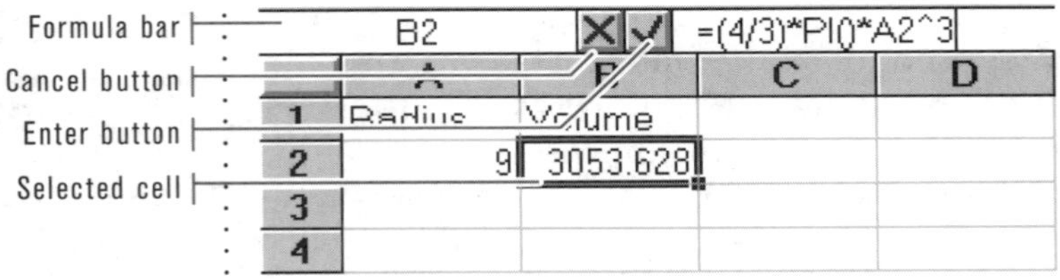

Figure 4-1. *To change a cell, select it and move the mouse cursor to the formula bar.*

Here's some handy cell editing skills:

- To move the cursor within the entry, click the mouse cursor where you want to place the cursor (or use the arrow keys).

- To add characters, move the cursor to where you want to add them and just start typing.

- To delete characters, press the Backspace key or the Delete key. Or just select the characters and type over the previous entry.

MOVING AND COPYING CELL CONTENTS

Similar to other Windows programs, Excel lets you use the Cut, Copy, and Paste commands from the Edit menu to move or copy a cell's contents and formatting.

But there's a much faster way. With Excel, you can use a drag-and-drop technique to move and copy cells. Here's how:

- To move the contents of cells, select the cells, use the left mouse button to select the outside border of the cells (hold down the mouse button), drag the cells to their new location, and release the mouse button.

- To copy the contents of cells, select the cells, hold down the Ctrl key, use the left mouse button to select the outside border of the cells (hold down the mouse button), drag the cells to where you want to copy them, and release the mouse button and the Ctrl key.

Copying selected characteristics of cells

You might want to copy a cell's value without copying the formula behind it. Or you might want to copy a cell's formatting without copying its values. You can use the Paste Special command from the Edit menu to copy only selected characteristics of a cell to other cells. With the Paste Special command, you can paste all of the cell's contents, only its formulas, only its values, only its formatting, or only its notes.

To copy only a single characteristic of cells, select the cells whose characteristic you want to copy and copy the selection to the clipboard (choose Copy from the Edit menu or press Ctrl-Insert). Then select the cells to which you want to copy the characteristic. Choose Paste Special from the Edit menu. From the Paste buttons, select the characteristic you want to copy and click OK.

For tools that make pasting the cell characteristics easier, see the sidebar "Toolbar tips" at the end of this chapter.

4

Adjusting formulas and values

With the Paste Special command, you can also adjust numbers or formulas that are off by a specific amount. Suppose a group of figures is off by the same number. For example, the sales tax (say 5%) was not added to the gross sales figures.

To adjust cell figures (values or formulas), type the adjustment value into an empty cell, select that cell, and choose Copy from the Edit menu (Figure 4-2). Then select the cells containing the figures, choose Paste Special from the Edit menu (Figure 4-3), and select Values from the Paste buttons. From the Operation list box, select how you want to combine the adjustment value. You can add, subtract, multiply, or divide the selected values by the adjustment value. Click OK.

Copy the adjustment value.

Select the values that need correction.

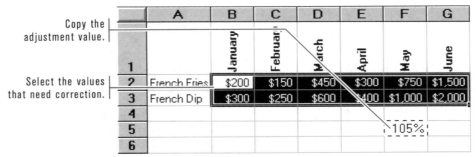

Figure 4-2. *To adjust the values in selected cells, use a combination of the Copy and Paste Special commands.*

Figure 4-3. *Select how you want to combine the adjustment value with the selected cells.*

	A	B	C	D	E	F	G
1		January	February	March	April	May	June
2	French Fries	$210	$158	$473	$315	$788	$1,575
3	French Dip	$315	$263	$630	$420	$1,050	$2,100
4							
5						105%	
6							

Figure 4-4. *Adjusted cells.*

DELETING AND INSERTING CELLS

So far, you've learned how to move the contents of cells. Moving actual cells is more complicated. You can't just remove cells and leave a blank spot on the worksheet. Likewise, you can't just drop new cells into a worksheet. Excel needs to move cells aside to make room for them.

Deleting cells

To remove cells from a worksheet, select the cells and choose Delete from the Edit menu. A dialog box appears asking you how Excel should close the space (Figure 4-5). Select Shift Cells Up to move up the cells below. Select Shift Cells Left to fill the space with the cells on the right. You can also choose to delete the entire row or column. Click OK.

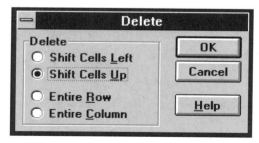

Figure 4-5. *When removing cells from a worksheet, you need to tell Excel how to fill the vacated space.*

Inserting cells

To insert new cells, select the number of cells you want to insert at the location you want to insert them. Choose Insert from the Edit menu. Excel will insert new cells into the worksheet, either by shifting down the current selection (and all the cells directly below it), or by shifting cells to the right, depending on which option you specify in the Insert dialog box. You can also insert entire rows or columns by selecting the Entire Row or Entire Column option in the Insert dialog box. When you're done, click OK.

> ### Fast editing
> Here are two speedup techniques that will save you from redoing tiresome editing tasks:
>
> - Repeat the last action. Choose Redo from the Edit menu to repeat an action. Excel even adds a word or two to the Redo command to remind you of what your last action was—such as Redo Insert.
>
> - Undo an action. Just as you can redo the last action you performed, you can undo what you did. Simply choose Undo from the Edit menu. Note that some complex actions are "undoable" so don't lean on this command too much.

FORMATTING WORKSHEETS

Now you're ready to custom build. With Excel, it's easy to format your worksheet to suit your needs and tastes. You can format numbers, alignment, text rotation, fonts, cell borders, column width and row height, and cell patterns.

Formatting numbers

What if a number, date, or time format isn't the one you want to use? Excel has over twenty built-in number formats for you to choose from. To change how values are displayed in selected cells, just click on the selection with the right mouse button and choose Number from the shortcut menu. The Number Format dialog box appears (Figure 4-6). You can view number formats by category by selecting a category in the Category list box or view them all by selecting All. From the Format Codes list box, select the format you want to use. Click OK.

If you have a number already entered in the active cell, the Sample section displays what it will look like.

Scroll here to select built-in formats   Look here to see how the number will appear

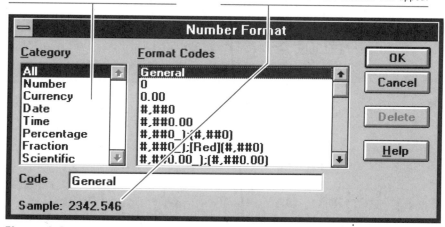

Figure 4-6. *You can change the number, date, or time format of the selected cells.*

In the Number Format dialog box, Excel uses the pound (#), zero (0), and question mark (?) to represent digits. These three placeholders represent different types of formatting for digits. For the standard formats, their differences won't matter too much—these differences only come into play for custom formats. To learn how to create custom number formats, see the next section.

Note that some of the Number and Currency formats have two number formats separated by a semicolon (;). For example:

```
#,##0_);[Red](#,##0)
```

The first format—#,##0_) in the example—is used to display positive numbers. The second format — [Red](#,##0) in the example — is used to display negative numbers. If you choose a format with the word Red in square brackets inserted before the number format (the negative format in the example), Excel will display the number format in Red. If you don't specify a negative format, Excel simply inserts a minus sign in front of the positive format to display negative numbers.

If the formats seem confusing at first, just remember to type the numbers into the cell *before* you do the formatting. That way you can see the results of a format option by looking at the Sample section.

EXAMPLE Try out some of the number formats yourself. Type a longer number such as 1234.567 into a cell. Click on the cell with the right mouse button and choose Number from the shortcut menu. Click on different formats in the list box and watch the results in the Sample section. This will help you learn the differences between the options.

The Number command affects only numbers, dates, and times. If you apply a number format to a cell containing text, the format won't take effect unless you replace the text with a number.

Restoring date formats
If you apply a numerical format to a date, the date changes into a mysterious 5-digit number. This is the stored value of the date. For example, the stored value of 4/21/1991 is 33349. Simply change the number format back to a date format to see the date displayed normally.

Creating custom number formats

If the built-in number formats don't suit you, you can create your own. Once you create a custom number format, it appears in the Number Format dialog box with the rest of Excel's built-in formats. You can apply custom formats just as you do the built-in formats.

To create a custom number format, select a cell where you want to apply the new format, click the cell with the right mouse button, and choose Number from the shortcut menu. From the Category list box, select the category you want to add the custom format to. In the Code text box, type the format code for the new format. Click OK.

What do you type for the format code? Number, date, and time formats have their own language. You use the letters *m*, *d*, *y*, *h*, and *s* to represent digits in dates and times. And you use special symbols such as #, 0, and ? to represent digits in numbers. You build a custom format by using these letters and symbols as placeholders for the actual digits in a cell entry.

Creating custom date and time formats

The m/d/yy code will make the date April 1, 1991 appear as 4/1/91. The letter *m* represents the digits for months, *d* for days, and *y* for years. You use groups of letters to specify the display format. For example, you can use a double *m* (mm) or double *d* (dd) to add leading zeroes to single-digit months or days (mm/dd/yy displays April 1, 1991 as 04/01/91). For a table of date digit formats, see Table 4-1.

To separate the date elements, you use the four common separator symbols: spaces, slashes (/), hyphens (-), or commas (,).

Essentially, time formats work the same as date formats—except that you always separate time elements with a colon (:). The letter *h* represents digits for hours, *m* for minutes, and *s* for seconds. Remember that Excel uses the 24-hour clock if you don't specify "AM/PM". For example, the format hh:mm a/p displays 4 o'clock pm as 04:00 p. Note that the you can abbreviate AM and PM to a/p or make it lowercase using am/pm.

4

Formatting worksheets

Table 4-1. *Date digit formats*

Digit code	Description	Example (using April 1, 1991)
m	month digit (no leading zero)	4
mm	month digit (leading zero)	04
mmm	month (three-character abbr.)	apr
mmmm	month (complete spelling)	April
d	date digit (no leading zero)	1
dd	date digit (leading zero)	01
ddd	day of week (three-character abbr.)	mon
dddd	day of week (complete spelling)	Monday
yy	year (two digit)	91
yyyy	year (complete digits)	1991

By using a date format such as mmmm, you can use actual dates as the headings for a row or column of dates and display only the month name. I suggest entering the date as the first day of the month (such as 1/1/93). By making the heading a date, you can easily expand the headings as a series. For more information on entering a series of dates, see Chapter 3.

Creating custom number formats

Suppose you need to deal with different types of currency (Yen and Pound) or different units of measurements (mm, hz, cc). Or what if you want to display values in the millions as millions (5 instead of 5,000,000)?

Here's how number formats work. The number zero (0), the pound symbol (#), and the question mark (?) represent digit placeholders. Their display is exactly the same if all places are filled. For example, the format codes 000, ###, and ??? all display the number 125 as 125. However, if there is no actual digit for the place, these three placeholders create different results:

■ The number zero displays a 0 (the format 000 makes 25 appear as 025).

- The pound symbol displays nothing (### makes 25 appear as 25).

- The question mark works the same way as the zero—except a leading space appears instead of a 0 so that the decimal points for all numbers with this format align.

You can also add text to a custom number format. Simply enclose the text within quotation marks ("*text*"). For example, the format 0.000 "cm" displays 1.4 as 1.400 cm.

You can add symbols such as ¥ (Yen) and £ (Pound) by typing the key combination (Alt-165 for ¥ and Alt-163 for £). For example, 0000 ¥ displays 10000 as 10000 ¥. If you don't know the key combination, use the Character Map program (CHARMAP.EXE) that comes with Windows 3.1 to find it.

You can also specify formats for different types of number entries: positive, negative, zero, and text. Recall the example at the beginning of this section:

```
#,##0_);[Red](#,##0)
```

This built-in format has two different formats for positive and negative numbers. The two formats are separated by a semicolon (;). Number formats follow this pattern:

Positive Format; Negative Format; Zero Format; Text Format

For example:

0.0;(0.0);"Null";"Invalid entry. Type a number"

In the example, positive numbers are displayed using the 0.0 format; negative displayed using (0.0); zero is displayed as the text "Null"; and any text entry is displayed with the text "Invalid entry. Type a number."

I've given you only some of the most handy custom formats—Excel lets you do many more.

4

> ### *Displaying 1,000,000 as 1*
> The thousands separator is a comma (,) and can be used for two effects. If you add a comma between two placeholders (such as the format #,#), Excel adds commas to separate thousands (1111111 is displayed as 1,111,111). If you place the comma after a placeholder with nothing following it (such as the format #,,), Excel suppresses a thousand for each comma (1111111 is displayed as 1). This can be handy when you're dealing with big numbers.

Aligning and rotating cells

By default, Excel formats text left aligned and numbers right aligned in a cell. And by default, both text and numbers are bottom aligned.

If you want to try something different, alignment is easy to change. Excel lets you display a cell's contents just about anywhere within the cell—you can control both its horizontal and vertical alignment. In addition, you can also rotate the values within the cell.

To adjust the alignment, select the cells whose alignment you want to change. Click on the selection with the right mouse button and choose Alignment from the shortcut menu. The Alignment dialog box appears, giving you alignment and text rotation (called *orientation*) options (Figure 4-7). Select the options you want. Then click OK.

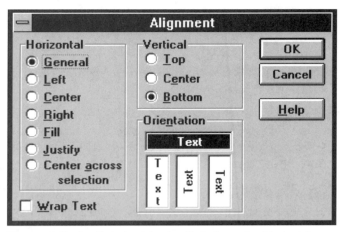

Figure 4-7. *Specify horizontal and vertical alignment and text rotation.*

The General alignment option formats cells with Excel's default alignment—numbers are right aligned, text is left aligned, both are bottom aligned.

The Left, Center, and Right alignment options are self-explanatory. Left alignment is often a good choice for row headings. Centered alignment is often used for column headings. And right alignment is the default choice for numbers, although some people use it for row headings, too.

It's also pretty clear what the Orientation buttons do. They let you rotate the values displayed within the selected cells. The text on these buttons show how the cell values will be rotated.

There are some other options that aren't as obvious. Here's a quick rundown:

- The Fill option repeats the contents of a cell until the cell is full. For instance, you might type an asterisk in a cell and then use Fill to make a star border that extends across the width of the cell.

- The Justify option lets you fit text into the area defined by the current selection so that it aligns evenly across the width of the selection.

- The Center Across Selection option centers a single cell's value across a group of selected cells (within a single row). To get this alignment effect, the cell that contains the text you want to center must have blank cells following it (that cell and the trailing blank cells make up the area where the text will be centered). Otherwise, Excel simply centers the text within each individual cell.

■ The Wrap Text option tells Excel to expand the height of the cell automatically so that all the characters you enter will appear in the cell. This ensures that all the text fits into the cell.

Rotate long headings...
... to gain horizontal space. Often, you have headings that are much longer than the values below. This means that you have a lot of wasted space in the cells that contain your values. To cram a few more cells on the screen, rotate the headings and tighten up the column widths (Figures 4-8 and 4-9). But make sure you leave enough column width for all your digits.

	A	B	C	D	E	F	G	H
1		January	February	March	April	May	June	
2	French Fries	$200	$150	$450	$300	$750	$1,500	
3	French Dip	$300	$250	$600	$400	$1,000	$2,000	
4								
5								
6								
7								

Figure 4-8. *Before rotating column titles.*

	A	B	C	D	E	F	G	H
1		January	February	March	April	May	June	
2	French Fries	$200	$150	$450	$300	$750	$1,500	
3	French Dip	$300	$250	$600	$400	$1,000	$2,000	

Figure 4-9. *After rotating column titles.*

Use Center Across Selection to group column titles
For instance, you can use this option to center a title over all the column titles. Or you can create a hierarchy of titles such as months grouped as quarters (Figure 4-10).

	A	B	C	D	E	F	G
1	Cashflow for High Anxiety, Inc.						
2		First Quarter			Second Quarter		
3	Jan	Jan	Feb	Mar	Apr	May	Jun
4	INFLOW						
5	Prev Month Balance	$10,000.00	$7,100.00	$4,400.00	$26,090.00	$79,369.00	$109,119.00
6	Interest/Investments	$1,000.00	$1,000.00	$1,000.00	$2,100.00	$1,000.00	$1,000.00
7	Product A	$2,500.00	$2,000.00	$5,000.00	$10,500.00	$5,000.00	$10,500.00
8	Product B	$3,000.00	$3,200.00	$3,090.00	$6,489.00	$3,090.00	$6,489.00
9	Product C	$600.00	$6,000.00	$12,000.00	$25,200.00	$12,000.00	$25,200.00
10	Misc	$7,000.00	$3,000.00	$14,000.00	$29,400.00	$29,400.00	$14,000.00
11	TOTAL INFLOW	$24,100.00	$22,300.00	$39,490.00	$99,779.00	$129,859.00	$166,308.00

Figure 4-10. *Use Center Across Selection to group columns into larger categories.*

Setting fonts

Changing fonts is handy when you're creating titles, headings, and summary lines. You can change the type style (called the *font*), size, attributes (called *style*), and color of the characters that are displayed within a cell. You can also add effects such as underlining and strikeout.

Excel handles fonts as most other Windows applications do.

To change the font, select the cells, click on the selection with the right mouse button, and choose Font from the shortcut menu. In the Font dialog box (Figure 4-11), select the Font, Size, Font Style, Effects, and Color. A sample of your final result appears in the Sample box. When you finish making your settings, click OK.

4

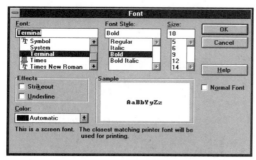

Figure 4-11. *Select the settings for the font.*

You can choose from three types of fonts:

■ *Printer fonts.* These are fonts that have been installed on the current printer (the one you've selected from either the Windows Control Panel or Excel's Page Setup dialog box). They appear in the Font list box with a printer icon next to them. These fonts may be on a cartridge or downloaded to the printer's memory. Unless you also have screen drivers for these fonts, Windows will display the closest screen font it has to display these fonts—so what you see on the screen may be close but not exactly what you print. In addition, you can't print these fonts on a printer that doesn't have them installed.

Font *faux pas*

It doesn't do much good to know how to operate the Font dialog box if you don't know what fonts to choose. Here are four dos and don'ts that will prevent you from committing the most common font *faux pas*:

- **Don't use more than two fonts in the same worksheet.** Use one for the titles and labels, and a second one for the numbers. Or use just one.

- **Do use serif and sans serif fonts together.** If you want two fonts in the same worksheet, choose one serif (such as Times Roman) and one sans serif (such as Helvetica). Don't mix two serif or two sans serif fonts together.

- **Don't vary font sizes too much.** Don't over-power the spreadsheet with huge fonts. A good, safe choice is to use 10-point type for the numbers, 12 or 14-point type for the headings, and 18 to 30-point type for the summary title at the top.

- **Do use bold to set off titles and totals.** You'll make your worksheet a lot more readable if you make only the key titles and totals bold.

- *TrueType fonts.* Windows 3.1 comes with a number of TrueType fonts. They appear in the Font list box with a True Type icon next to them. TrueType fonts accurately display on the screen what you get when you print. In addition, the font information is stored in the document that uses the font (such as a worksheet), so no matter what printer you use the fonts will print—as long as it's a printer supported by Windows.

- *Screen fonts.* These fonts are used for screen display only and a printer font is substituted when the document is printed. No icon appears next to these fonts.

What fonts should you use? TrueType is the most portable and provides an exact match between screen display and printed output. However, more printer fonts (such as Bitstream and Adobe Postscript) are currently available than TrueType—although more and more TrueType fonts will probably become available. But it doesn't matter how many fonts are available if you don't use them wisely. For some guidelines, see the sidebar "Font faux pas."

Shortcuts for formatting fonts

The Normal check box applies the Normal style's font, style, color, effects, and size. Pressing Ctrl+1 applies the Normal font to a cell. Pressing Ctrl+2 turns boldface on and off. Pressing Ctrl+3 turns italic on and off. Pressing Ctrl+4 turns underline on and off.

Formatting cell borders

When you open a new worksheet, all the cells have dotted gridlines to show their borders. You can change the color and pattern of any or all of the four borders (top, bottom, left, and right). You can use cell borders to group cells, separate cells, or just get attention.

To change cell borders, select the cells, click the selection with the right mouse button, and choose

Border from the shortcut menu. The Border dialog box appears (Figure 4-12). From the style boxes, select the Style. From the Color list box, select a color. Then click on the Borders to which you want to apply the Style and Color. When you finish setting up the borders, click OK.

Figure 4-12. *Select the Style, Color, and placement (Border) of borders.*

The Style section has eight boxes with different border patterns. To select a style, click on the box that contains the pattern you want.

The Border boxes let you apply the border style you've just selected to any of the four borders or all of them. The Outline option applies the border around the outside of the selection—not around each cell in the selection. To have four borders around each cell in the selection, apply the border to Top, Bottom, Left, and Right.

To remove a border, click on the border's Border box so that no line appears in the box.

The Color list box lets you change the color of the border. Don't bother changing the color unless you happen to have a color printer, or if you just want to make a section easier to find on the screen. Colors print as a shade of gray on normal printers.

The Shade check box applies color shading that you can adjust with the Patterns command from the Format menu.

Controlling column width and row height

When you open a new worksheet, all the cells have a standard width and height. When cell values are too big to fit within the default cell size. Excel will either display values in exponential format, display only part of the text, or fill the cell with pound signs (#).

You can adjust column width and row height so that all cell contents will show. To adjust the width of a column, place the mouse cursor on the right border of the column head. The cursor becomes a vertical line with two horizontal arrows. Drag the column border until the cell is the size you want. To adjust the row height, drag the bottom border of the row heading. For more details on adjusting column width and row height to fit the cell contents, see Chapter 3.

Formatting cell patterns

Like cell borders, cell patterns can be formatted to highlight important data, separate titles from data, or group cells together. The *cell pattern* is the pattern and colors of the area inside a cell.

To change cell patterns, select the cells, click the selection with the right mouse button, and choose Patterns from the shortcut menu. The Patterns dialog box appears, giving you different pattern and color options (Figure 4-13). When you've chosen your settings, click OK.

4

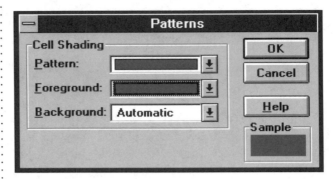

Figure 4-13. *Select the pattern and color of the area within cells.*

The Pattern drop-down list box lets you pick a pattern. If you select "solid" (second from the top of the list box), the Foreground color will fill the selected cells. If you select a pattern, the Foreground color becomes the color of the dots or lines and the Background color serves as the background for the foreground patterns. You can see a sample of the pattern you've created in the Sample box.

FINDING, REPLACING, AND SPELL-CHECKING

4

Excel gives you some editing tools that you've probably used in your word processor:

- The Find command searches for specified characters or numbers that occur within formulas and values on the worksheet.

- The Replace command searches for specified characters or values and replaces them with others.

- The Select Special command selects all cells containing a specified type, such as formulas, blank cells, constant values, and so on.

Finding characters or numbers

You need to find data before you can edit it or format it. It's easy on a small worksheet. But on a big worksheet, you won't want to scroll through screens and screens of cells. The Find command lets you search for specified characters or numbers that are either stored or displayed in cells.

To find characters or numbers, specify the cells you want to search. You can search the whole worksheet (select a single cell—Excel then searches from that cell to the end of the worksheet) or just the current selection (select the cells to search). Then choose Find from the Formula menu. The Find dialog box appears (Figure 4-14). In the Find What entry box, type the characters or numbers you want to search for. To specify how to search, select the search options you want. Click OK.

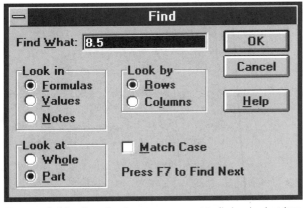

Figure 4-14. *Type the characters you want to find and select how to find them.*

For finding, numbers are just characters

When you type a number in the Find What entry box, Excel treats that number as a string of characters; and when it searches the worksheet cells, it looks at the values and formulas that are stored and displayed as characters—not as the text, numbers, and formulas they really are. This means when you search for 8.5, Excel tries to find a match for the string of characters 8.5.

4

You can tell Excel how to search. Here are the most important options:

- The Formulas button searches for characters or numbers that are within the values or formulas stored in the cells—not necessarily the displayed values. For example, you could search for the value 8.5 (or a value with 8.5 within it, such as 268.53). Excel would find it in a cell with the formula =8.5*C7 but not in a cell with the formula =4.25*2 (which evaluates to and displays as 8.5).

- The Values button searches for characters or numbers that are displayed in cells—not necessarily the stored values. For example, if you did the same search for 8.5 as in the previous example, Excel wouldn't find =8.5*C7 unless the formula evaluated to 8.5 or a value with 8.5 within it.

- The Whole button searches for an exact match for the characters in the Find What entry box. For example, if you search for 8.5, Excel finds only the cells that have the value equal to 8.5, not values that contain 8.5 within the value, such as 58.57.

- The Part button searches for cells that contain the specified characters anywhere within the cells. Excel finds such values as 8.525 and 18.5 as well as just plain 8.5.

- The Rows button tells Excel to move across rows when searching.

- The Columns button tells Excel to move down columns.

- The Match Case check box lets you find characters that match the case (uppercase and lowercase) exactly. To match the case, enable this check box. For example, if you search for Mac, Excel finds the cells with that exact capitalization and won't find the same characters that don't, such as mac or MAC. To find all matching characters regardless of case, disable this check box. Usually you'll want to have this option disabled.

Switching the direction of search
Excel searches forward by default (across from left to right and top to bottom). You can search in the reverse direction by holding down the Shift key when you click OK in the Find dialog box.

Finding cells fast
To find the next cell containing characters you want, press F7. To find the previous cell, press Shift-F7.

Replacing text

Sometimes you need to replace a specific number, word, or group of characters with another. The Replace command works almost exactly as the Find command does.

To replace characters, specify the cells you want to search in. You can search the whole worksheet (select a single cell—Excel then searches from that cell to the end of the worksheet) or just the current selection (select the cells to search in). Then choose Replace from the Formula menu. The Replace dialog box appears (Figure 4-15). In the Find What entry box, type the characters you want to replace. In the Replace With entry box, type the characters that you want to replace the Find What characters. To specify how to do the replace, select the search options you want (they work the same way as the Find command options). If you click Replace All, Excel replaces all instances of the Find What characters with your Replace With entry. If you click Find Next, Excel finds the next instance, and then you have the option of clicking Replace to replace just that instance or move on to the next instance by clicking Find Next again. Click Close when you're done.

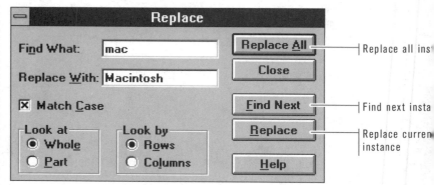

Replace all ins⌐

Find next insta⌐

Replace curren⌐
instance

Figure 4-15. *Type the characters you want to find and the ones to replace them with, then select how to find them.*

Finding specific types of contents

Often you want to find certain types of contents such as formulas that display errors, constant values, or blank cells. Excel can select these special types of contents for you so you can find them easily.

To select types of contents, specify the cells where you want to look for the types (works just like finding or replacing) and choose Select Special from the Formula menu. The Select Special dialog box appears (Figure 4-16). Then select the type you want to find. Click OK.

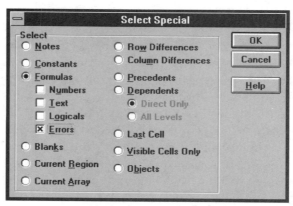

Figure 4-16. *Select the type of cell contents you want to find.*

> ### *Finding cells that are referenced*
> Before you edit or delete cells, it's good to know if other cells refer to those cells or if those cells have references to other cells. Here's how to find these references:
>
> ■ To find cells that refer to the cells within a selection (a single cell or group of cells), select the referenced cell(s), choose Select Special from the Formula menu, and select the Dependents button. Click OK. All the cells that contain references to the cells within the original selection are selected.
>
> ■ To find cells that the cells within the selection refer to, follow the same steps as above except select the Precedents button. All the cells that the cells within the selection have references to are selected.

FAST FORMATTING

You don't have to go through all the formatting steps you've learned in this chapter for every cell in your worksheet. There are three ways to avoid repeating your formatting labors—or even to avoid them all together:

■ *Cell styles* to store cell formatting and apply it to other cells

■ *AutoFormat* to apply standard table formats to a group of cells instantly

■ *Templates* to retain data, formatting, and formulas for a worksheet and use them as the starting point for new worksheets

Using cell styles

Once you've set the formatting for a cell, you can easily reapply it to other cells—without having to redo your settings again. Excel has *styles* that let you store the formatting you've applied to a cell, give it a name, and apply that format to other cells.

To use styles, select a cell, apply the formatting you want, and click in the Style list box in the Standard toolbar—it's at the far left and probably shows "Normal" (the default Normal style). Delete the text in the Style list box, type the style name you want, and press Enter. Now the style can be applied to any cell.

To apply a defined style, select the cells and select the style from the Style drop-down list box.

Using AutoFormat

If you prefer, you need not create any fancy formatting—you can pick one of Excel's standard table formats and apply it to the selected cells. Then all the number, border, font, pattern, alignment, column widths, and row heights will be applied for you.

To apply a table format, select the cells you want to format (Figure 4-17), choose AutoFormat from the Format menu, select a format from the Table Format list box (Figure 4-18), and click OK. The selected cells now have the selected table format (Figure 4-19).

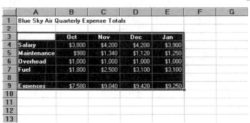

Figure 4-17. *Select the cells to format as a table,...*

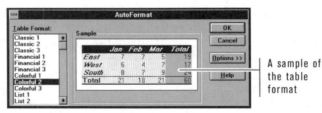

Figure 4-18. *...Select a table format,...*

	A	B	C	D	E	F	G	H
1	Blue Sky Air Quarterly Expense Totals							
2								
3		Oct	Nov	Dec	Jan			
4	Salary	$3,800	$4,200	$4,200	$3,900			
5	Maintenance	$980	$1,340	$1,120	$1,250			
6	Overhead	$1,000	$1,000	$1,000	$1,000			
7	Fuel	$1,800	$2,500	$3,100	$3,100			
8								
9	Expenses	$7,580	$9,040	$9,420	$9,250			
10								
11								
12								
13								

Figure 4-19. *. . . Then the cells are formatted as a table.*

In the Sample box, you get a sample of what the table format looks like. By clicking the Options button, you can apply only some of the format for a standard table—just disable the ones you don't want. By default, all formats are applied.

Creating templates

You can spend a lot of time customizing a worksheet to suit your needs. (You can also create them for charts—see Chapter 5.) You don't want to have to start over if you want to use the same formatting for a new worksheet. In Excel, you can create worksheet templates that already have the data, formatting, or formulas you want to use (Figure 4-20).

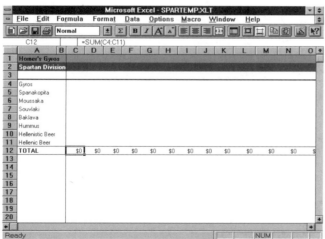

Figure 4-20. *You can create a worksheet template that has all the formatting you need to use as a starting point.*

To create a template, simply create a worksheet you want to use as a starting point for a new worksheet. Choose Save As from the File menu (Figure 4-21). Save the template in the XLSTART subdirectory of the Excel root directory (the directory where Excel is installed). Type a filename for the template in the File Name text box. You don't have to give the filename an extension. Excel automatically gives templates an XLT extension. Select Template from the Save File As Type list box. Click OK. To enable the template, choose Exit from the File menu and restart Excel.

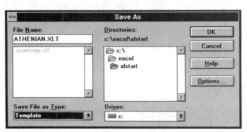

Figure 4-21. *Save the worksheet as a Template (Save File As Type) and place it in the \XLSTART subdirectory.*

To use a template as a starting point for a new worksheet, choose New from the File menu. The New dialog box appears with the names of templates in the list box (Figure 4-22). Double-click on the template name you want to use.

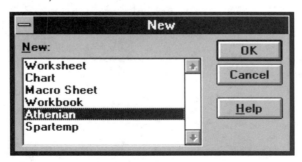

Figure 4-22. *When you choose New from the File menu, templates appear in the New list box.*

You can also use the Open command from the File menu to open a template file. The template itself doesn't open. A new worksheet is created with the template just as when you use the New command from the File menu. If the template is not in the XLSTART directory, the Open command is the only way to create a new worksheet from a template.

If you want to make changes to a template, hold down the Shift key, choose Open from the File menu, navigate to the appropriate directory, and double-click on the template's filename (it should have the XLT extension). The template file will open and you can edit it as needed.

N ow that you've learned how to make your data stand out with custom formatting, I'm going to show you how to enhance it graphically using Excel's charting features. Turn to the next chapter to learn how.

Toolbar tips

Add these handy tools to your toolbar to make
editing and formatting a snap:

Editing

The **Paste Formats tool** lets you paste only
the format of the copied cells.

The **Paste Values tool** lets you paste only the
values of the copied cells.

The **Clear Formulas tool** removes only the
values or formulas stored in the selected cells. The
formatting remains intact.

The **Clear Formats tool** removes only the
formatting applied to the selected cells. The values or
formulas remain intact.

The **Check Spelling tool** lets you check the
spelling of text in the cells of the current worksheet.
If you're a Word for Windows user, you'll find that
Excel's spellchecker works pretty much the same way.

Formatting

B **I**   The **Bold** and **Italic tools** are already on the Standard toolbar—but they'd be a useful addition to a custom toolbar. The Bold tool makes the cell values bold; the Italic tool makes them italic.

The **Alignment tools** (Left Align, Center Align, and Right Align) are also standard equipment. These tools have left-, right-, or center-aligned lines on them that show you exactly what they do.

The **Increase Font Size tool** applies the next larger font size in the current font. The **Decrease Font Size tool** applies the next smaller font size. These tools are also on the Standard toolbar.

The **Orientation tools** (Vertical Text, Rotate Text Up, and Rotate Text Down) let you rotate the cell values. Pick one and stick to it; otherwise, you (or whoever uses your worksheet) may twist your head off trying to read your worksheet.

4

4

The **Text Color tool** lets you change the color of the cell values–another tool to use sparingly. Remember that a single-colored cell value in a mass of black cell data is an eye-catcher; colored cell values peppered across the whole worksheet are just distracting.

The **Decimal tools** (Increase Decimal and Decrease Decimal) let you add and remove decimal places from the formats of selected cells. Each time you click one of these tools, you add or remove one decimal place. Note that this affects only the displayed format–not the actual values contained in the cells.

The **Percent Style tool** makes the values in selected cells appear as percentages. Note that this won't make the value 75 appear as 75% (it will display as 7500%). To make percentages appear correctly, the cell values must be entered as the proper decimal value for percentages (75% should be entered as .75).

The **Currency Style tool** lets you apply the default Windows currency format to the values in selected cells. In the United States, this is the dollar sign ($). If you have specified another country in the International dialog box in the Windows Control Panel, the symbol of a bill and coins may appear in the Customize dialog box instead of the the dollar sign.

CREATING CHARTS AND WORKSHEET GRAPHICS

Usually, your worksheet must be more than a repository for information. You need to use your information to make a point. With Excel, you can present your analysis succinctly with a chart or use worksheet graphics to call attention to important information. In this chapter, you'll learn how to convert worksheet information into charts and dress it up with worksheet graphics.

CREATING CHARTS

The most dramatic way to present your information is with a chart. Charts make it easy to compare data and see trends.

If you've already tried creating a chart with multiple rows and columns of data, you know it's confusing at first. Excel's chart terminology can be mind-boggling. In this section, you'll get a grip on that terminology. Then I'll give you the skills you need to create and handle charts:

■ How to create charts the easy way with Excel's ChartWizard—make a chart with five fast steps.

■ How to create and use chart templates.

■ How to edit the format of charts.

■ How to rotate 3-D charts.

■ How to use the tools on the Charting toolbar.

Understanding chart terminology

Before you create charts, you need to know Excel's chart lingo. It's easy to look at a chart and recognize its parts. But it isn't always easy to remember Excel's names for those parts. To get a handle on Excel's chart terms, take a look at Figure 5-1.

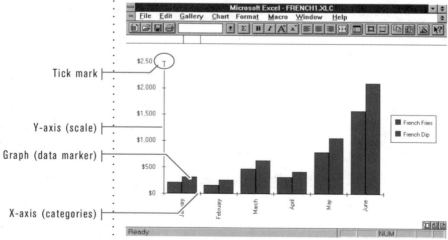

Figure 5-1. *Excel's chart terminology.*

Excel charts have two axes—a horizontal X-axis and a vertical Y-axis. Normally, the X-axis contains different categories, while the Y-axis is a scale of values.

You can tell Excel how to plot the data (Figure 5-2). You can specify to have the column headings appear as the graphs (the months in FRENCH2.XLC) and the rows appear as labels for the graphs (French Fries and French Dip in FRENCH2.XLC). Or you can specify the row headings (French Fries and French Dip in FRENCH1.XLC) as the graphs and label them according to the column headings (the months in FRENCH1.XLC). When Excel converts data to charts, it usually represents rows as categories along the X-axis, and columns as a series of graphs (bars on a bar chart, lines on a line chart, and so on).

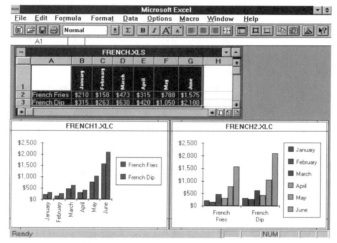

Figure 5-2. *You can plot data in two ways.*

As you can see in Figure 5-2, the same data gets plotted (twelve bar graphs). They simply are labeled and grouped differently. Excel has its own unintuitive terminology for the graphs and labels:

■ The individual graphs (each plotted bar, point on a line, pie slice, and so on) are called *data markers*.

■ Each series of graphs is called a *data series*. A data series is a set of graphs that represent a specific item (such as French Fries and French Dip in

FRENCH1.XLC). For a column chart, the graphs in a data series have the same color and pattern. For a line chart, the data series is a single plotted line (that is, the set of all the plotted points for the line). However, it may be simplest to think of a data series as whatever is represented by the legend. The *legend* shows what each color column (or what each color line) represents (such as French Fries and French Dip in FRENCH1.XLC).

■ The labels for the graphs on the X-axis (tick marks on a line chart, the grouping of bar columns on a column chart, labels for pie slices on a pie chart, and so on) are called *categories*.

Selecting the data for the chart

Before you create a chart, you need to select the cells containing the data you want to plot on the chart (Figure 5-3).

When selecting the cells to chart, follow these rules:

■ Make sure that the values are the same type (all dollar values, all percentages, and so on).

■ Make sure that the selected cells can be combined into a rectangular block. This means you can select noncontinuous cells—but they should be sets of cells that have either the same number of rows or the same number of columns. Usually, you'll select a continuous rectangular block of cells.

Excel can use the first row and column as special labels for the chart. It uses them to create names for each set of graphs (data series) to use on the legend and to create X-axis labels. You can pick whether to use them for these two labeling purposes or you can plot one of them as the first series in the chart.

Making the most of charts

To get the most impact from a chart, remember its strengths in presenting information. Here are some tips:

- **Simplify information**. A chart summarizes information. So don't clutter it with zillions of categories. It's much easier to compare two or three items than 20 or 30.

- **Show change.** Charts show trends and cycles best. A chart showing little variation in its values isn't an eye-catcher, and probably isn't informative either. If the variation of values is significant, but doesn't show up in the chart, change the scale to make the variation more noticeable. (You change the scale by changing the start or step values of the Y-axis.)

- **Show relationships.** For example, a pie chart works best for showing the relationship of a piece of data to the whole.

- **Use words to help readers.** Have you ever looked at the laundering instructions for a shirt? The tag has strange symbols (one looks like a caldron of acid), and you're never quite sure what they mean. Pictures are great, but use labels to make sure readers get your intended meaning.

- **Tilt 3-D line charts to exaggerate change.** You can make the lines on a line chart look steeper or flatter by rotating the chart. In Figure 5-13, the line chart is tilted up to make the line seem steeper. This is a dirty trick—but I know you won't abuse it.

5

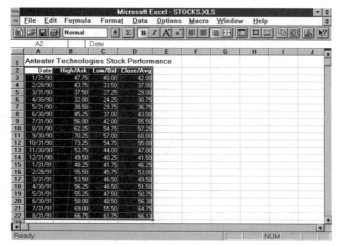

Figure 5-3. *Before you create a chart, you need to select the cells to chart.*

Generating charts

After you've selected the data, there are two main ways to generate a chart:

■ Use the ChartWizard tool.

■ Use a chart template.

Chart templates are easier and faster if you've already set up a chart template to use. But if you're starting from scratch, the ChartWizard is a simple, step-by-step way to create a new chart.

After you've generated a chart, you may need to add, change, or delete data from your worksheet. Don't worry. You won't have to start over again. The chart and the worksheet data are linked, so that changes made in the worksheet are automatically reflected in the chart.

Using the ChartWizard

Rather than having to set up every element of a chart, you can use the ChartWizard tool on the Standard toolbar (the button with a bar chart and wand) to specify only the essential settings. If you need to make adjustments, you can fine-tune the chart later.

To create a chart with the ChartWizard, select the cells containing the data you want to chart and click the ChartWizard tool. Then place the cursor on the worksheet where you want to place the upper-left corner of the chart and drag until the dashed box is the size you want for the chart. Then you specify how to build the chart by stepping through five dialog boxes.

Here's how to get through the five steps:

1. *Confirm that you have the correct cells selected.* The first dialog box (Figure 5-4) simply asks you to confirm that you've selected the cells you want for the chart. If the selection is the one you want, click Next to move on to the next step. If it's not right, you can edit the reference in the Range box—but it might be easier to click Cancel and reselect the cells.

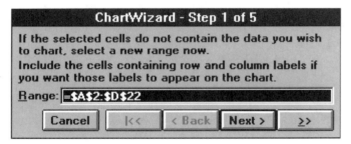

Figure 5-4. *Click Next to tell Excel you've selected the right cells.*

2. *Select the type of chart.* In the second dialog box (Figure 5-5), you specify the type of chart you want. Click on the chart's picture. The chart's picture will be highlighted. From this step on, you will see the options for the type of chart you've selected. Click Next to move to the next step. You can return to this step from a later one by using the Back button to move back.

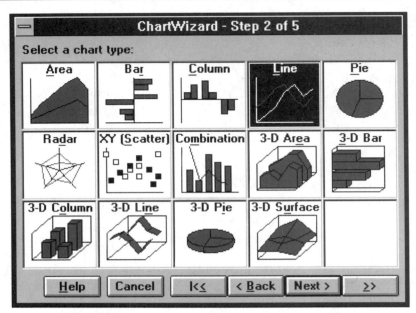

Figure 5-5. *Pick the chart type by clicking on its picture (a line chart is selected here).*

5

3. *Select the format of the chart.* In the third dialog box (Figure 5-6), you select the format of the chart. The dialog box displays the formats available for the chart type you selected. Click on the picture of the chart with the format you want. Click Next to move to the next step.

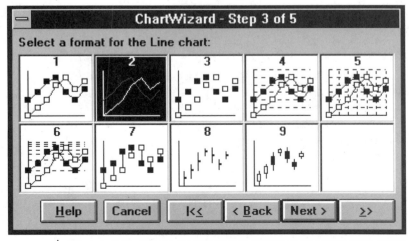

Figure 5-6. *Pick the chart's format by clicking on the picture of the format.*

4. *Specify how the data is placed into the chart.* In the fourth dialog box (Figure 5-7), you see a preview of your chart in the Sample Chart box. You also specify how you want your cell data plotted on the chart. Usually, Excel picks the settings you'll want. So most of the time, you'll just leave these settings alone and click Next to move on to the next step.

But if data isn't in the right place, here are your options:

- The Data Series In buttons let you choose whether to plot graphs (lines, areas, bars, points, surfaces, or pie slices—depending on the type of chart you picked) for each row or for each column. In the legend in the Sample Chart box, you see the sets of graphs (which Excel calls data series) that are plotted on the chart. By default, Excel plots what you have fewest of (rows or columns). Usually, the default is what you want. In Figure 5-7, there are fewer columns than rows so the columns are plotted.

- The second group of buttons can either be Use First Column For or Use First Row For, depending on the Data Series In setting. These buttons let you choose whether to use the first column (or row) of cells as the labels for the X-axis (Category (X) Axis Labels) or plot them as a graph (First Data Series).

- The third group of buttons has the title that the second group doesn't (Use First Column For or Use First Row For). These buttons let you choose whether the first row (or column) provides the text for the chart's legend (Legend Text) or is used as the first point plotted in each data series (First Data Point).

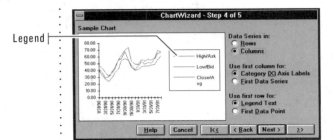

Legend

Figure 5-7. *Pick how to plot your cell data.*

5. *Add a legend, chart title, and axes labels.* In the fifth (and last) dialog box (Figure 5-8), you specify whether the chart has a legend and create a title and axes labels. To add a legend, select Yes for Add A Legend?. To create a title, type the title text in the Chart Title text box. To create labels for the axes, type the label text in the appropriate Axis Titles text box (Category (X) and Value (Y)). In the Sample Chart box, you'll get a preview as you type the text (Figure 5-9). Click Next to create the chart. The chart appears in the space you defined with the dashed box you drew earlier (Figure 5-10).

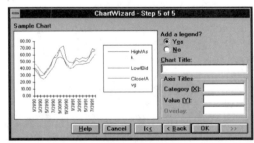

Figure 5-8. *By default, Excel adds a legend but no title or axes labels.*

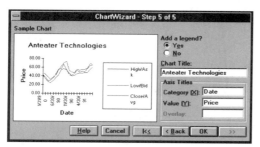

Figure 5-9. *The Sample Chart box shows a preview of how the chart will look with legend, title, and axes labels.*

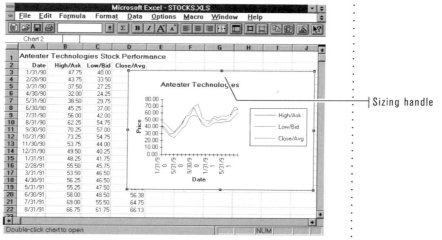

Sizing handle

Figure 5-10. *After you've completed the five steps, the chart appears on the worksheet.*

What you've just created is an *embedded chart*. This type of chart is part of the worksheet. When you save the worksheet, you save the chart with it. When you print out the worksheet, the chart prints with it.

You can size the chart by dragging the sizing handles—just like any other Excel graphic. For more information on sizing graphics, see the next section "Using worksheet graphics."

To save the chart as a separate document, make sure that the chart is in an active window (double-click on an embedded chart). Then use the Save command from the File menu.

Using chart templates

The second way to generate a chart is with a chart template. Chart templates let you select the data you want to plot and create a chart document using the format you saved in the chart template. But before you use a chart template to create a new chart, you need to create the template.

To create a chart template, create or open a chart that has the format that you want and make sure that the chart is in its own active window (if it's an embedded chart, double-click on the chart). Choose Save As from the File menu. In the File Name text box, give the chart template a name. In the Save File As Type list box, select Template. In the Directories box, navigate to the XLSTART subdirectory of the directory where you installed Excel (usually, C:\EXCEL\XLSTART). Click OK. Now the chart template will appear in the New list box when you use the New command from File menu.

To use a chart template, select the cells containing the data you want to chart and choose New from the File menu. In the New list box, select the chart template. Click OK. The chart appears with the chart format defined in the template. The chart appears in its own document window and is not embedded on the worksheet.

To save the new chart as a document, make sure that the chart is in an active window. Then use the Save command from the File menu.

To embed the new chart on a worksheet, activate the chart's document window, choose Select Chart from the Chart menu, and choose Copy from the Edit menu. Then switch to the worksheet's document window, select the cell where you want to place the upper-left corner of the chart, and choose Paste from the Edit menu.

> ***Give chart templates distinctive filenames***
> Give chart templates filenames that distinguish them from
> worksheet templates. I start the filenames of my templates
> with the letters "ch" so I can easily pick them out from regular
> worksheet templates in the New list box.

Editing charts

After you've created a chart, you can adjust its format
to suit your needs. When a chart's window is active, a
special set of menu items appears in the menu bar.
The Gallery, Chart, and Format menus contain commands that let you format charts. In this section, you'll
learn these chart handling skills:

- Selecting types of charts with the Gallery commands

- Adding, selecting, and removing chart elements

- Adjusting the format of chart elements

    Before you can work with a chart, you need to place
it in its own document window.

    To open a chart in a document window, double-
click on it if it's an embedded chart. To return to the
worksheet but leave the chart's window open, choose
the worksheet's filename from the Window menu. To
close the window, double-click the window control
button in the upper-left corner of the chart's document window.

Changing the type of chart

    There are two main types of charts: two-dimen-
sional and three-dimensional (3-D). With the commands on the Gallery menu, you can choose any chart
type you want. You can select from 90 different variations of 14 kinds of charts (Figure 5-11).

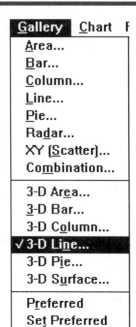

Two-dimensional charts

Three-dimensional charts

Figure 5-11. *Use the commands on the Gallery menu to select the type of chart you want.*

Don't be blown away by all the choices. In essence, there are only six kinds of charts: column, line, pie, scatter, radar, and surface charts. For most things, column, line, and pie charts are all you'll ever need. Everything else is just a variation. (If you have a practical use for a scatter, radar, or surface chart, you probably already have a good idea of how to use them.)

A bar chart is simply a horizontal column chart. An area chart is a shaded, adjusted line chart. And a scatter chart is another type of line chart. Excel offers 3-D versions of all these chart types except scatter charts.

Certain types of charts show certain types of data best:

■ Pie charts are best at showing how a piece relates to the whole—especially percentages (Figure 5-12).

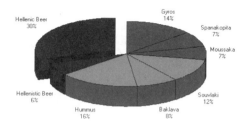

Figure 5-12. *Pie charts show how a piece relates to the whole.*

■ Line charts are best at showing trends and directions (Figure 5-13).

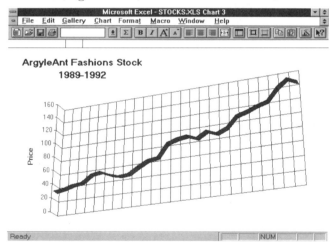

Figure 5-13. *Line charts show direction (falling or rising values) and continuity (values following a trend).*

■ Column charts are best at comparing multiple series of data. Excel can group graphs in categories for easy comparison (Figure 5-14).

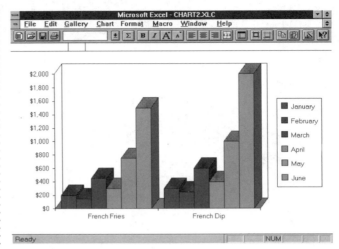

Figure 5-14. *Column charts make it easy to group data in categories for easy comparison.*

To change the type of chart, make sure that the chart's document window is active. Then choose the chart type from the Gallery menu (Figure 5-11). The dialog box for that chart type appears displaying the variations. Click on the picture of the variation you want. Then click OK to apply the new chart type to the active chart.

Cycling through chart types
Use the Next and Previous buttons to cycle through the chart types. After you've chosen a chart type from the Gallery menu and the dialog box appears, check out what the other types have to offer by clicking on the Next and Previous buttons. This way you won't have to close the dialog box and return to the Gallery menu.

Adding chart text
As you learned earlier in this chapter, you can add axis labels to the chart. However, you can also attach additional text. If you haven't added text for a title, the axes, or series, you can do it now.

To add a title, axes labels, or series labels, choose Attach Text from the Chart menu. In the Attach Text

To dialog box, choose the type of text you want to add. Click OK. A text box appears on the chart containing the generic term for the type of text you selected. For example, if you chose Chart Title, a box containing the word *Title* appears above the chart. Type the text in the formula bar and press Enter. The text appears on the chart.

You can format chart text created with the Attach Text command, but you can't move it. Excel moves and sizes the text, using its own criteria to make it fit. For instance, Excel automatically centers chart titles and places them above the chart's plot area. Excel also automatically places text labelling axes, series, and series values.

Sometimes, you need to position text by hand. For example, callouts need to point out the exact item they're labelling. And Excel can't always make the axes and series labels for 3-D charts fit correctly—they can bump into each other.

Don't worry, Excel lets you create text that can be sized and moved around the chart. This type of text is called *unattached text*.

To create unattached text, first make sure the whole chart is selected (click outside the plot area and make sure the word Chart appears in the reference area). Type the text in the formula bar, and press the Enter key. The text appears on the chart with black sizing handles around it. You can drag the text to any position on the chart. Or use the sizing handles to change the shape of the box containing the text.

Formatting chart text

To format chart text, simply click on the text with the right mouse button, choose the format you want to change from the shortcut menu, and make the changes in the dialog box.

Formatting chart elements

To format a chart element (such as the bars on a bar graph, or the scale on the Y-axis), simply click on the element with the right mouse button, choose the format you want to change from the shortcut menu,

5

and make the changes in the dialog box. Each chart element has slightly different options, such as border, area, scale, fonts, and text.

When you select an element, white selection handles appear around it. The reference area displays the name of the chart element you selected (Figure 5-15).

Reference area
Selection handle

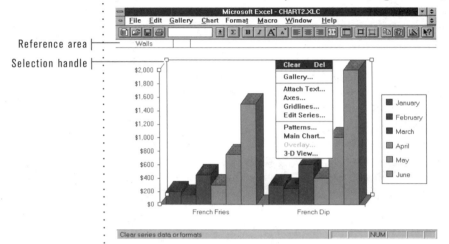

Figure 5-15. *Click on a chart element with the right mouse button to open a shortcut menu.*

Using Excel charts in other applications

For those of you who prefer working with Windows drawing applications such as CorelDRAW! or Arts & Letters, you can use the clipboard to copy a chart from Excel and paste it into the application. You can also import them into an image editor such as the Windows Paintbrush.

Adjusting the number range on the scale axis

All charts (except pie charts) have an axis with a scale of values. By default, Excel gives enough range for the values on the vertical axis to ensure that all the cell data is plotted. However, you may want the values to start or end at a different value. Or you may want a different step value between tick marks. All these settings control the vertical axis *scale* of the chart. Note that on a two-dimensional chart the vertical axis is the Y-axis and on a 3-D chart the vertical axis is the Z-axis.

To adjust the vertical axis scale of an active chart, click the axis with the right mouse button (make sure the axis name appears in the reference area, usually Axis 1 for the Y-axis) and choose Scale from the shortcut menu. The Scale dialog box appears. Make the changes you want. Click OK.

Here are the handiest options:

■ To set a new start value, delete the value in the Minimum entry box and type the new start value.

■ To set a new end value, delete the value in the Maximum entry box and type the new end value.

■ To set a new step value for the major units (usually these are the tick marks displayed), delete the value in the Major Unit entry box and type the new major step value. You can also specify a minor unit (the tick marks between the major unit tick marks).

Rotating 3-D charts

3-D charts add another dimension to charts. And Excel lets you view 3-D charts from any side. It's simple to rotate 3-D charts.

To rotate a 3-D chart, make sure the chart is in its own active document window and click on one of the eight corners of the chart. Black rotation boxes appear at the chart's corners and Corners appears in the reference area (Figure 5-16). Click on one of the rotation boxes and hold down the mouse button. Drag the rotation box to rotate the chart. Excel displays only the outline of the chart while you are rotating it (Figure 5-17). Release the mouse when you have the chart in the position you want. The chart appears on the screen.

5

Creating charts

Reference area

Rotation handle

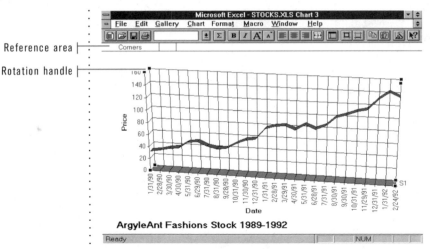

ArgyleAnt Fashions Stock 1989–1992

Figure 5-16. *When rotating a chart, make sure that Corners appears in the reference area.*

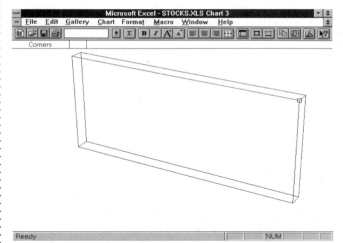

Figure 5-17. *When you drag the rotation handles, the chart is displayed with only its outline.*

Using the chart tools

There are some handy tools that make creating and editing charts faster and easier. You can open the Charting toolbar (Figure 5-18) or add the chart tools you use most often to your custom toolbar.

Figure 5-18. *The Charting toolbar is the fast way to many chart commands.*

You'll recognize the pictures on the first seventeen tools—they are the specific variations of charts. You can create the chart displayed on the tool by selecting the cells to chart, clicking on the tool you want, and dragging a box on the worksheet to draw the chart. If you have a chart open, you can switch to a chart type by clicking on the tool with the format you want.

Here's how the other chart tools work:

 The **Preferred Chart tool** lets you use a defined chart format to create a chart or format a chart. To define a chart format as preferred, make sure the chart whose format you want to use is in an active document window and choose Set Preferred from the Gallery menu. You can apply this format to any chart by activating the chart and choosing Preferred from the Gallery menu. To create a chart using the preferred format, select the cells you want to chart, click the Preferred Chart tool, and draw the chart.

 The **ChartWizard tool** lets you create a chart in five easy steps (see "Using the ChartWizard" earlier in this chapter).

The **Horizontal Gridlines tool** turns the gridlines for the axes on or off.

The **Legend tool** adds or removes a legend.

The **Arrow tool** draws an arrow.

The **Text Box tool** adds unattached text to the chart.

Break out of your cell! You can enhance the look of your worksheet with more than just cell borders and patterns. Excel has graphic tools that let you draw on a worksheet. The basic drawing tools that you find in your favorite drawing or paint application are right there on the Drawing toolbar: the Line tool, Oval tool, Rectangle tool, Arc tool, and Polygon tool. Each tool is represented by a button with the appropriate shape on it (Figure 5-19).

Figure 5-19. *The Drawing toolbar has many of the tools you find in most popular draw programs.*

In this section, you'll get the essentials for drawing graphics on a worksheet:

- How to draw graphics (lines and shapes)
- How to edit graphics (size, move, and delete them)
- How to format graphics
- How to handle multiple graphics at once
- How to stick electronic Post-It Notes on a worksheet
- How to capture an image of what appears on screen

Drawing graphics

To draw a graphic, click on the appropriate drawing tool on the Drawing toolbar. For example, if you want to draw an oval, click on the Oval tool (the button with the oval on it). The cursor turns into a crosshair. Position the cursor where you want the shape to begin.

Drag the mouse until the shape is the size you want, and release the mouse button.

Have you drawn your guns but decided not to shoot? If you select a tool and decide not to use it, press the Esc key.

Perfect drawing
To create a "perfect" line or shape, hold down the Shift key while drawing. Using this method, you can make lines snap to 45-degree angles, draw squares with the Rectangle tool, draw circles with the Oval tool, and draw an arc as a perfect "slice" of a circle.

Gridline snap
To force lines or shapes to snap to cell gridlines, hold down the Alt key while drawing, moving, or sizing them.

Sizing, moving, and deleting graphics

As with cells, you must select a graphic before you can do anything with it. Simply click on the graphic, and *sizing handles* appear around it.

To size a graphic, drag a sizing handle until the shape is the size you want.

To move a graphic, click inside it and drag it to its new position. If you prefer, you can select the graphic and choose Cut from the Edit menu to place it on the clipboard. Click on the worksheet at the new position, and choose Paste from the Edit menu. Cutting and pasting is the best way to move a graphic long distances (across multiple screens, for example) or to another worksheet. Dragging works best for fine-tuning the graphic's position.

To copy a graphic, select it, choose Copy from the Edit menu, click on the worksheet where you want to place the copy, and choose Paste from the Edit menu.

To delete a graphic, select it and choose Cut from the Edit menu.

Formatting lines and shapes

Formatting the shapes you create with Excel's graphic tools is like choosing jelly donuts at a bakery: you pick the shape and the filling inside. Lines are simplest: they don't have filling. We'll talk about lines first.

Formatting lines

You can control two characteristics of a line: its body (the line) and its end style (an arrowhead, for example) (Figure 5-20).

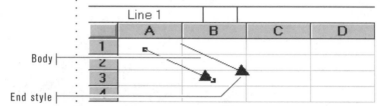

Figure 5-20. *The two characteristics of a line.*

To format a line, double-click on it. The Patterns dialog box opens (Figure 5-21). Use the options in the Line box to adjust the Style, Weight (thickness), and Color of the line's body. Use the options in the Arrow Head box to adjust the end style of the line. Click OK to apply the selected format to the line. In the Sample box, Excel shows you a preview of how the line will look on the worksheet.

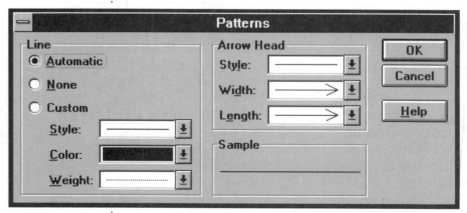

Figure 5-21. *Make formatting changes to lines with this dialog box.*

When you draw a line, Excel gives it the default body and end style—a solid, narrow line with no arrowheads. When you first open the Patterns dialog box, the Automatic button is selected. By selecting Automatic, you apply the default body style.

Selecting None makes the line invisible, but what's the point?

By selecting the Custom button, you can use the Style, Color, and Weight list boxes in the Line box to give the line the pattern, color, and thickness that you want.

Formatting shapes

Formatting shapes is similar to formatting lines. Double-click on the shape. The Patterns dialog box appears. You format the border surrounding the shape the same way you format a line. If you click on Shadow, Excel will create a shadow behind the shape's border. If you have a rectangular shape, click on Round Corners to make its corners rounded.

The Fill box contains options for formatting the inside of the shape. The Automatic button gives a shape the default white fill. The None button gives the shape no fill, making it transparent. If you select the Custom button, you can specify your own pattern, foreground color, and background color for the selected shape. Click OK when you've made all your changes.

The Sample box gives you a preview of the results of your selected options.

Working with multiple worksheet graphics

You can work with multiple worksheet graphics to create special effects such as callouts or logos. Excel gives you these features to handle multiple graphics:

- Changing the stacking order of graphics that overlap each other.

- Combining multiple graphics into one single graphic.

Changing stacking order

If you have overlapping graphics, you can change their stacking order. Think of overlapping graphics as a deck of cards. If you want to change their stacking order, use the Send To Back and Send To Front commands.

To move a graphic behind the others, select the graphic and choose Send To Back from the Format menu.

To move a graphic to the top layer, select it and choose Send To Front from the Format menu.

Combining graphics

After your placement of multiple graphics is just right, you want to move them as a single group. You can combine multiple graphics into one group.

To combine graphics, first select all the graphics you want to group by clicking on the Selection tool in the Drawing toolbar (the button with the rectangle with dashed lines). The cursor turns into a crosshair. Position the cursor where you want to begin the selection. Drag across the area that contains the graphics. Any graphic inside the dashed line is included in the selection—even if only part of the graphic lies inside. Choose Group from the Format menu. Now you can select, size, and move the whole group at one time.

To break up a combined group, select it and choose Ungroup from the Format menu. The graphics are now separated with sizing handles around each one.

> ### *Electronic Post-It Notes*
> Ever wish you could put electronic Post-It Notes on your worksheet or chart? With the Text box tool, you can draw a box on the worksheet and type text inside it. You can combine text boxes and lines to create callouts for important information.

Capturing pictures of the screen

Sometimes for presentation purposes, you need to show part of a worksheet. You can use the Camera tool to take a "picture" (make a copy) of any group of cells on a worksheet or any part of graphics or charts embedded on the worksheet. This picture can be moved or sized.

The picture is linked to the original worksheet so that changes to the original data are reflected in the picture.

To create a picture, select the cells you want to "photograph," click on the Camera tool in the Utility toolbar (button with the camera), and then click on the worksheet where you want to place the upper left corner of the picture. The picture appears in the same size and proportion as the original cells.

To size the picture, drag the sizing handles around the picture. As you adjust the size, the picture's size relative to the original is displayed in the reference area as a percentage. For example, 65% X 75% means that the width is 65 percent of the original and the height is 75%. Try to maintain the original proportions. Otherwise, Excel may cut or distort the picture.

In this chapter, you learned how to enhance a worksheet with charts and worksheet graphics. In the next chapter, you'll learn how to print what you've done.

5

5

CHAPTER 6

PRINTING

This may be the age of electronic information, but nothing is more convincing or powerful than the printed page. In this chapter, I'll show you how to print all of your hard work so you can show it off to your colleagues.

After you install a printer in Windows, you can use it to print an Excel document. If you haven't installed a printer yet, you must do so with the Printers option in the Windows Control Panel. For information on installing printers, see the Windows documentation.

You follow five steps for printing:

■ Select a printer

■ Select the area to print

■ Switch to Print Preview (optional)

■ Set up the page layout

■ Print the document

SELECTING A PRINTER

You need to select a printer only if you want to use one different from the Windows default. To select a printer, choose Page Setup from the File menu. The Page Setup dialog box appears and displays the current printer. Click the Printer Setup button. The Printer Setup dialog box lists installed printers (Figure 6-1). Select a printer from the Printer list box. Click OK twice. Now you can print to the selected printer.

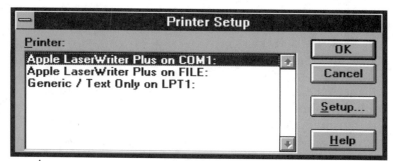

Figure 6-1. *Select a printer in the Printer Setup dialog box.*

To adjust the printer settings (such as paper size) for the current document only, don't use the Setup button in the Printer Setup dialog box. Instead, use the Page Setup dialog box options (Figure 6-2). These settings are saved with the current document, but won't affect printer settings of other Excel documents or other applications—with one exception: If you save a group of Excel documents as a workbook (more on workbooks in Chapter 7), Page Setup changes for one document affect all the documents in that group.

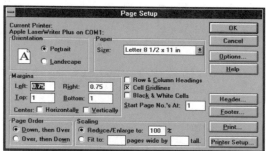

Figure 6-2. *Make printer settings for individual documents in the Page Setup dialog box.*

To adjust the printer settings for *all* Windows applications, click the Setup button within the Printer Setup dialog box. A dialog box with the printer's name appears. This is the same dialog box that you see when you set up a printer with the Windows Control Panel. The changes you make here affect the printer settings for all Windows applications—not just Excel.

SELECTING THE PRINT AREA

Excel lets you print only a few rows or columns. Simply select the cells and choose Set Print Area from the Options menu. Dashed lines indicate borders of the print area (Figure 6-3), which Excel names "Print_Area." Now only selected cells will print, along with worksheet graphics within the selected area.

To print the whole worksheet again, click the Select All button (Figure 6-3) and choose Remove Print Area from the Options menu.

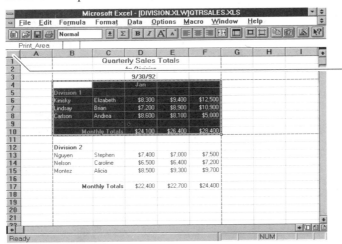

Select All button

Figure 6-3. *The print area is surrounded by dashed lines.*

SWITCHING TO PRINT PREVIEW

The claim to fame for most Windows applications is their ability to show on-screen what you get when you print. In Excel, you can get a rough idea of the printed page by choosing the Print Preview command from the File menu (Figure 6-4).

Click here to view
the next page

Click here to view
the previous page

Click here to open the
Page Setup dialog box

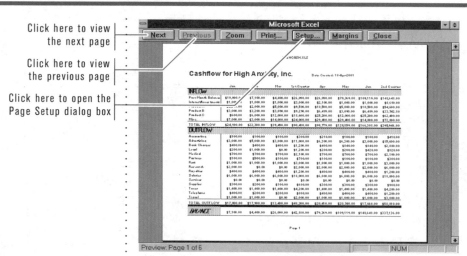

Figure 6-4. *Use Print Preview to see how Excel will print the worksheet on the page.*

When you're setting up page layout...

...work in Print Preview mode so that you can see the results of your changes. In addition, all the printing commands are available at a click of a button. Make life easy for yourself and use Print Preview to fine-tune printer settings and page layout.

In Print Preview mode, the cursor turns into a magnifying glass if you move it onto the page. To see an enlarged view, position the magnifying glass over the area you want to see and click the mouse button once (Figure 6-5).

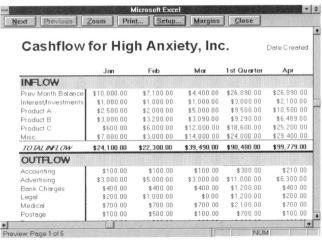

Figure 6-5. *Enlarged view of a page in Print Preview mode.*

To zoom back out to full-page view, click once anywhere on the page.

To go to the previous page, click the Previous button. To move to the next page, click the Next button.

To go back to the regular view of the document, click Close.

SETTING UP PAGE LAYOUT

With the Page Setup dialog box, you can control the page layout of a worksheet. First, switch to Print Preview mode so you can see a preview of the printed pages. Open the Page Setup dialog box by clicking the Setup button (Figure 6-6). (This is the same dialog box that opens when you choose Page Setup from the File menu.)

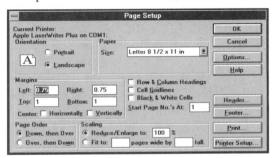

Figure 6-6. *Use the Page Setup dialog box to control page layout.*

Whether you're printing a worksheet, a macro sheet, or a chart, you can control the following basic elements in the Page Setup dialog box:

- The width of page margins

- The content and format of headers and footers

- Whether to show row and column headings and gridlines on the printed page (worksheets and macro sheets only)

- The sizing of worksheets and charts on the printed page

- The orientation and size of pages

- The page sequence

Note that the capabilities of your specific printer may determine whether or not you have some or all of these page setup options.

Setting margins

You can set page margins by typing numbers in the Page Setup dialog box. But there's an easier way if you're in Print Preview mode.

You can set page margins quickly and easily by choosing Print Preview from the File menu and clicking the Margins button. The margins appear as dotted lines with sizing handles at the edge of the page (Figure 6-7). To change a margin, drag the sizing handle. The status bar displays the width of the margin as you drag. Note that adjusting a margin affects *all* pages, not just the current page.

To set margins in the Page Setup dialog box, choose Page Setup from the File menu and type the margin widths in the Left, Right, Top, and Bottom text boxes. You can also center the document (that is, the cells, graphics, or charts that Excel has been able to fit on the page) within the margins by using the Center check boxes. To center the document vertically, enable the Vertically check box. To center horizontally, enable the Horizontally check box.

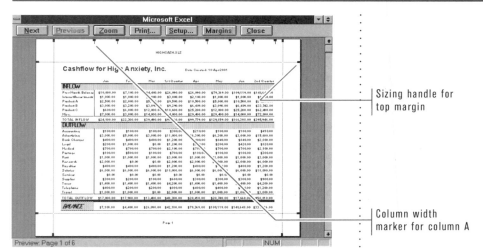

Figure 6-7. *To enlarge or reduce the width of a margin, drag the sizing handle for the margin.*

To size column widths, drag the column width marker for the column you want to size. The column width marker represents the right border of the column.

Creating headers and footers

You can also add headers and footers to each page. To add a header to each page, open the Page Setup dialog box and click the Header button. The Header dialog box appears (Figure 6-8). To add a footer, click Footer instead; the Footer dialog box works the same way as the Header dialog box. Type the text in the appropriate Section text boxes. Click OK twice.

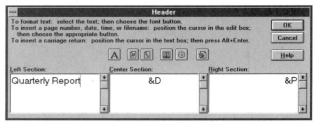

Figure 6-8. *Type the header text in the Section text boxes.*

In headers and footers, you can have groups of text that are aligned to the left, center, or right (Figure 6-9). You simply type the text in the appropriate Section text box (Left Section, Center Section, Right Section). For example, to left align the text "Quarterly Report," center align the current date, and right align the page number, you type Quarterly Report in the Left Section text box, &D in the Center Section, and &P in the Right Section (Figure 6-8).

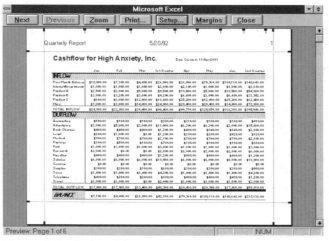

Figure 6-9. *Header and footer text can be placed on the left, center, or right side of the page.*

In the example, the codes &P and &D are used as placeholders for the page number and date. When you print the worksheet, these codes are printed as the actual page number (&P) and date (&D). By default, Excel uses the filename as the header and the page number as the footer.

You can use other codes to further customize your headers and footers. Header and footer codes begin with an ampersand (&), followed by a letter, a number, or both. You can use these codes to apply special values specific to the current document. Table 6-1 lists the header and footer codes. The letters in the codes are capitalized, but it won't matter if you type them in lowercase. You can also have Excel insert these codes for you by pressing the appropriate tool button—but it's easier for me to remember the first letter of the special text I want to insert (such as &D for date) than to remember what the icons on the buttons mean.

Table 6-1. *Header and footer codes*

Code	Description
&D	Prints the current date.
&T	Prints the current time.
&F	Prints the filename.
&P	Prints the page number.
&P+*number*	Adds the **number** to the current page number and prints the new number.
&P–*number*	Subtracts the **number** from the current page number and prints the new number.
&N	Prints the total number of pages in a document.

You can also format the fonts for each Section. To format the Section text, select the text and click the Font tool. The Font dialog box appears (this is the same dialog box you used to format cell fonts). Make the font settings. Click OK. For more information on setting fonts, see Chapter 4.

Press Shift-Enter for line breaks

Although the Section text boxes appear to wrap text automatically to the next line, Excel does not automatically wrap Section text. You must manually break lines by using a Shift-Enter where you want a Section line to break. Otherwise, the text for the three sections may overlap.

Avoiding header and footer overlap

Excel always places headers in an area 0.5 inches from the top edge of the page and 0.75 inches from the sides of the page. Likewise, footers are placed 0.5 inches from the bottom edge and 0.75 inches from the sides of the page. The margin settings have no effect on the header and footer placement. However, if the margins are too small, the document may overlap the header or footer.

Adjusting starting page numbers
Use the &P+*number* and &P-*number* codes to adjust the starting page number. For example, if you're printing a report that begins on the second page (the first page is a cover sheet), use the code &P-1 to make the page number on the second page begin with 1.

Hiding gridlines and row and column headings

To prevent gridlines and row and column headings from printing, disable the Cell Gridlines and Row & Column Headings check boxes (make sure there's no X mark in them) in the Page Setup dialog box. Disabling them in Page Setup won't affect how they display.

Sizing worksheets

The Scaling group in the Page Setup dialog box lets you set the size that the active worksheet prints when it's printed. There are two ways: (1) by specifying a percentage of the original size or (2) by specifying the number of pages to fit the whole worksheet.

Here's how:

■ To size the worksheet by percentage, select the Reduce/Enlarge To button and type the percentage that you want to reduce or enlarge the original in the % entry box. For example, to reduce the size to one-quarter of the original size, type 25. To enlarge the size to double the original size, type 200. The default size is 100%.

■ To size the worksheet by compressing the worksheet to fit on a specific number of pages, select the Fit To button and enter the numbers in the Pages Wide By and Tall entry boxes.

Sizing charts

When you're adjusting the page setup for a chart, Excel disables the worksheet-specific buttons and boxes (such as the Row & Column Headings check-box) and adds the Chart Size buttons (Figure 6-10).

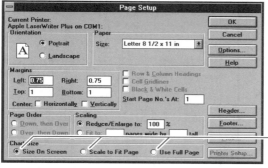

Size buttons

Figure 6-10. *The Page Setup dialog box is slightly different for a chart.*

Here's what the Chart Size buttons do:

- The Use Full Page button sizes the chart so that it fills the area within the page margins. Excel does not maintain the exact proportions (the ratio of width to height) of the chart as it appears in a document window. Excel will stretch the chart to fit the page so the chart may look distorted.

- The Scale To Fit Page button sizes the chart to fit the area within the page margins. Excel makes the chart as large as possible but still maintains the proportions of the chart as it appears in the document window.

- The Size On Screen button prints the chart at the same size and proportions that it appears in the document window.

Setting page orientation and size

Depending on your printer, Excel may enable two more convenient options for you in the Page Setup dialog box. They let you set the page orientation and size for the active document. These options are generally available on PostScript printers. As with the other Page Setup options, these do not affect the general printer settings for all Windows applications. Here's how they work:

- The Orientation buttons allow you to set the page orientation for an individual document to Portrait (tall) or Landscape (wide). Worksheets often fit better when printed in landscape orientation. This option appears for most Hewlett-Packard LaserJet printers too, not just PostScript printers.

- The Paper list box allows you to select the paper size for a document. This option is handy if you usually print on 8½ x 11 standard letter size, but need the extra length or height of 8½ x 14 legal size paper for large worksheets.

Setting the page sequence

In a long worksheet, there are usually more rows and columns than you can legibly print. Excel automatically defines the page boundaries for you—it fits as much as it can on each page using the settings in the Page Setup dialog box. The page boundaries are displayed on the screen as dashed lines. You can tell Excel the sequence in which to print these defined pages with Page Order buttons in the Page Setup dialog box. Here's what the two buttons do:

- The Over, Then Down button prints pages going across the worksheet left to right then moves down to the next set of pages and so on.

- The Down, Then Over button prints pages going down the worksheet top to bottom then moves to the right to the next set of pages and so on.

Repeating Titles on Every Page

Often, you have columns of data that are many pages long. To keep track of the data, you need to repeat the column titles on each printed page.

To set repeating column titles, select the entire row containing the column titles (click on the row heading), choose Set Print Titles from the Options menu.

The Set Print Titles dialog box appears. Do not adjust the settings. Click OK.

You can use the same technique for row titles—except you select the entire column containing the row titles.

If you want to have both repeating row and column titles, select the row containing the column titles, hold down the Ctrl key, select the column containing the row titles, choose Set Print Titles from the Options menu, and click OK.

To turn off the print titles, click the Select All button and choose Remove Print Titles from the Options menu.

U sually, Excel doesn't divide pages exactly the way you want. For example, you may want to keep certain types of information together on one page. Don't worry, you're not stuck with Excel's page breaks. You can set manual page breaks.

To set a manual page break, select the cell immediately below and to the right of where you want the page break. Then choose Set Page Break from the Options menu. A dashed line indicates the page boundaries (Figure 6-11).

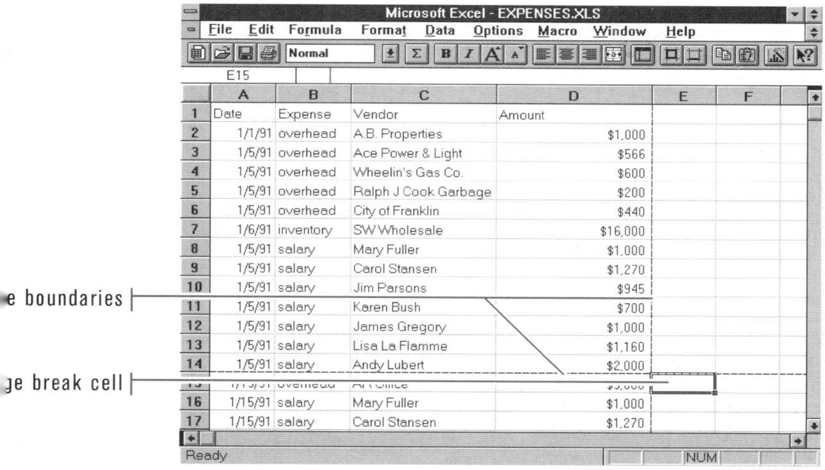

SETTING PAGE BREAKS

6

e boundaries

je break cell

Figure 6-11. *Setting page breaks.*

To remove a page break, select the cell you used to set the page break (if you can't remember, it's the cell outside the lower-right corner of the page boundary). Then choose Remove Page Break from the Options menu. The dashed page boundary disappears.

PRINTING DOCUMENTS

After you set up your preferred printing options, you can print your worksheet or chart. This is the easy part.

To print the active document, choose Print from the File menu (or if you're in Print Preview mode, click on the Print button), type the number of copies you want in the Copies text box, select the specific pages you want to print with the Print Range option, and click OK.

In the previous chapters, you learned how to get your data into a worksheet, format it, and analyze it. In this chapter, you learned how to print all your hard work. Next, you'll find out how to link worksheets together so that when you make changes in one worksheet, another worksheet will automatically be updated. You'll also learn how to group worksheets, macro sheets, and charts together.

Toolbar tips

Here are some tools that will help you get to the printing commands faster:

 The **Print Preview tool** switches Excel to print preview mode.

The **Set Print Area tool** sets the current selection as the print area.

The **Print tool** prints the active document.

CHAPTER 7

LINKING INFORMATION

Linking information in Excel is like watching a magic trick; it seems amazing until you know how it works. But even then, this Excel feature is so useful you'll want to experience it over and over again. You've already learned how to use cell references to link from one cell to another within the same worksheet. But you can go beyond the confines of a single worksheet.

There are four ways to create a link between documents:

- Make a linked copy of cells from other worksheets.

- Create formulas that refer to cells on other worksheets.

- Export data to other applications.

- Handle Excel documents as a single group.

In this chapter, I'll show you these four linking features.

CREATING A LINKED COPY OF CELLS

In Excel, you can link cells in one worksheet to cells in another worksheet. Linking saves you the hassle of updating changes to worksheets that share values or have calculations that depend on values in other worksheets.

For example, suppose you have three worksheets that record monthly income and you want to summarize the data in another worksheet that displays income for the first quarter (Figure 7-1). You want a way to display and use the monthly totals in a separate summary worksheet—and you want the summary worksheet to be automatically updated with any changes to the individual monthly worksheets.

Too much to ask? Excel makes it almost as easy as copying cells.

To place a linked copy of cells from one worksheet to another worksheet, make sure both the source and destination worksheets are open (for an explanation of source and destination worksheets, see the sidebar "Source and destination worksheets"). Select the cells that you want to link in the source worksheet and copy the cells (click on the selection with the right mouse button and choose Copy from the shortcut menu). Next activate the destination worksheet and select the cell that will be the upper left corner of the range of cells that will contain the linked cells (make sure there's enough room for the linked cells). Choose Paste Link from the Edit menu. Now the destination worksheet contains a linked copy of the cells from the source worksheet (Figure 7-1).

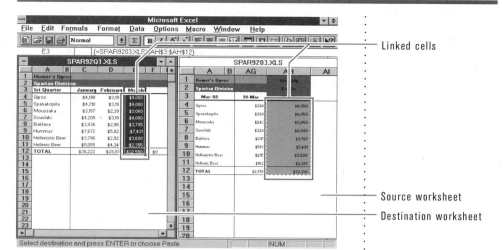

Figure 7-1. *In Excel, you can link data from one worksheet to another.*

> ### Refer to linked cells by name
> In the source worksheet, define a name for the range of cells you want to link. For example, if you linked a range of cells that contained the sales totals for March, you might name that range March_Totals. By naming linked cell ranges, you'll be able to identify their contents easily and to select them quickly using the Goto command from the Formula menu.

Controlling links

After you've created links between worksheets, you may have to find, update, move, or sever those links. In this section, you'll learn how.

Navigating back to the source

It's easy to backtrack from the destination worksheet to the source document. Simply double-click the destination cells and Excel will navigate back to the reference. Excel will activate the source worksheet (Excel will open it first if it's not open), go to the source cells, and select them.

7

Renaming and moving linked worksheets

With all of the source and destination worksheets open, you can rename source worksheets or move them to a new directory. Excel will automatically update the links with the new name and location.

However, if the destination worksheet isn't open and you change the name or location of a source worksheet, Excel won't update the link. Excel will look for the old filename in the old location and won't be able to find the source worksheet.

To make sure your source and destination worksheets can successfully link, follow these rules:

- Save the source documents *before* you link them to other worksheets.

- Have all linked worksheets (source and destination) open when you rename or move them.

- Rename linked worksheets using the Save As command from the File menu in Excel. Moving or renaming a closed destination worksheet with a file utility (such as File Manager or a DOS command) may disconnect the link.

- Keep linked worksheets in the same directory.

Source & destination worksheets

The term "linking" is a little misleading because you can't make direct changes to the linked cells from both sides of the link. You must make changes to linked cells at the *source* worksheet where those cells were originally located. The *destination* worksheet contains a linked copy of the cells from the source worksheet. Changes to values and formulas in a linked cell must be made in the source worksheet. (For more on getting back to the source worksheet, see the section "Controlling links" in this chapter.) However, you can make any formatting changes you want to the linked cells on the destination worksheet.

What should you do if you've moved a source worksheet where Excel can't find it? The simplest solution is to move the file back. However, you can also redirect the link to the new location.

To redirect a link to another source worksheet, activate the destination worksheet and choose Links from the File menu. The Links dialog box appears (Figure 7-2). The Links list box displays all of the source worksheets for the active destination worksheet. Select the source worksheet whose link you want to redirect. Click the Change button. The Change Links dialog box appears (Figure 7-2). Use the Directories list box to navigate to the new directory. In the Files list box, select the filename of the new source worksheet. Click OK. Then click Close. The links for the original source worksheet have been redirected to the new source worksheet.

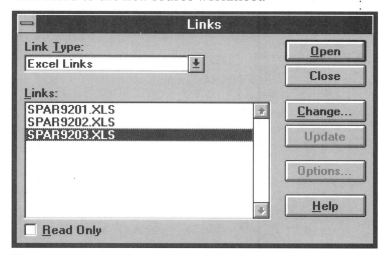

Figure 7-2. *Select the link to redirect and click Change.*

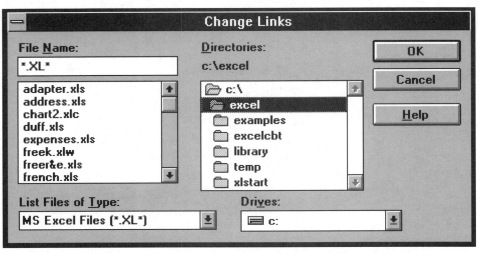

Figure 7-3. *Select the file you want to redirect the link to and click OK.*

Severing links

Severing links is simple. You can eliminate a link in two ways:

- Clear everything out of the destination cell.
- Sever the link but keep the current values.

> **When severing links...**
> ...make sure you've selected every cell in the linked range. You cannot sever the link of just a cell or two. If you select only part of the range, Excel gives a "Cannot change part of an array" message. Why? When you selected a range of cells to link to another worksheet, Excel linked all of the selected cells as one big group.

To sever a link and delete the values at the destination cells, activate the destination worksheet, select the linked cells, and choose Clear from the Edit menu. The Clear dialog box appears (Figure 7-4). To clear everything from the selected cells, select the All button. To clear only the linked values from the selected cells but keep the formatting, select the Formulas button. Click OK.

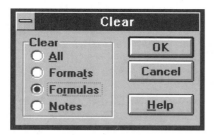

Figure 7-4. *Select the All button or the Formulas button to clear the links and their values.*

To sever links but keep the values in the destination cells, activate the destination worksheet, select the linked cells, and choose Copy from the Edit menu. A marquee appears around the selected cells. Choose Paste Special from the Edit menu. The Paste Special dialog box appears (Figure 7-5). From the Paste buttons, select Values. From the Operation buttons, select None. Be sure that the two check boxes at the bottom are disabled (no X in the box). Click OK. Now the selected cells are no longer linked to the source worksheet—but the values remain as constants.

Figure 7-5. *To sever links and convert the linked values to constants, select the Values button.*

CREATING FORMULAS USING LINKED REFERENCES

You don't always need to link cell to cell. You may only need to include a value from another worksheet within a formula. There are two ways to refer to cells on other worksheets:

- Select the cells in the source document.

- Type the cell reference directly into the formula.

The selection technique is the simplest.

To create a formula that refers to cells in another worksheet, begin typing the formula in the destination worksheet. When you need to refer to the cells in the source worksheet, activate the source worksheet and select the cells to be referenced. Switch back to the destination worksheet, finish typing the formula, and press Enter to store the formula (Figure 7-6).

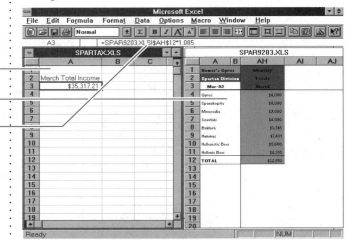

Destination worksheet

Source worksheet

Formula

Figure 7-6. *In your formulas, you can refer to cells on other worksheets.*

As you can see in Figure 7-6, Excel refers (from within formulas) to cells on open source worksheets using the following form:

source filename! *absolute cell reference*

For example, a reference to the cell AH12 in the open worksheet SPAR9203.XLS would look like this:

    SPAR9203.XLS!$AH$12

If you do not have the source worksheet open, you need to include the full path and enclose the path and filename within single quotation marks. Our example would look like this:

```
'C:\TEMP\SPAR9203.XLS'!$AH$12
```

Needless to say, it's easier to use the selection technique. But this knowledge isn't totally useless. Once you've made the reference, it may be easier to edit the cell reference (for example, if the reference is off by one cell and you've closed the source worksheet) than redo them with the selection technique.

7

Linking to Other Applications

Sometimes, you need to use Excel data and graphics in other Windows applications (or vice versa). For instance, you might want to use an Excel chart in a report written in Microsoft Word for Windows. Or you might want to add a graphic created in CorelDRAW! to an Excel worksheet. You have several options:

- Use Excel data in other Windows applications without linking it.

- Link Excel data to documents in other Windows applications.

- Link data in other Windows applications to Excel.

- Export data as a file.

- Export charts as a file.

Linking to Windows applications

The Windows environment makes it easy to exchange data and graphics between Windows applications (such as Excel, Word for Windows, CorelDRAW!, and many more). Creating a link between another application and Excel is almost as easy as linking between Excel worksheets.

Note that the other application must know how to handle Excel objects (such as cells or charts). Check the application's documentation to make sure that it can link with Excel. Excel objects can link with other applications only if the other application supports Windows and Dynamic Data Exchange (DDE).

To use Excel data in another Windows application without linking it, select the Excel objects (cells or a chart) you want to link. Then choose Copy from the Edit menu to place a copy of the data on the clipboard. Switch to the other application. In the document in that application, place the cursor where you want to insert the Excel data. Choose Paste from the Edit menu. The item appears in the document (Figure 7-7).

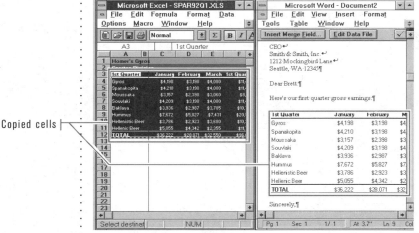

Figure 7-7. *You can copy data from Excel and paste it into other Windows applications such as Word for Windows.*

There are two ways to link a source document in another Windows application to a destination worksheet in Excel. The easy way is to use the Paste Link command from the Edit menu and using the same procedure I showed you for linking Excel worksheets together.

You can also go the other direction.

To link a source worksheet (or chart) in Excel to a destination document in another Windows application, select the worksheet, select the object you want to link (cells or chart), and choose Copy from the Edit menu. Activate the destination document in the other application. Follow that application's method for creating links. For example, in Word for Windows you would choose Paste Link from the Edit menu.

Exporting data as files

There's another way to export Excel data to other applications without using the clipboard. This lets you move Excel data to DOS applications (such as dBASE). In most cases, you can save Excel data as a file that's compatible with the other application. In Excel, you can save worksheets in many common file formats.

To save a worksheet in a different file format, activate the worksheet and choose Save As from the File menu. The Save As dialog box appears (Figure 7-8). In the File Name text box, type a new filename. From the Save File As Type list box, select the type of file format. Excel will give the file an extension that is common for the file format (for example, DBF for dBASE files). Click OK.

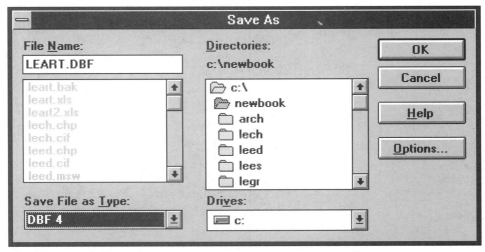

Figure 7-8. *Give the worksheet a new filename and format.*

The file formats listed in the Save File As Type list box may look cryptic to you. However, you may be able to recognize the one that you need by its file extension.

For example, the common extension for Lotus 1-2-3 is WKS and for dBASE is DBF. The numbers following the extensions are version numbers (DBF 4 for dBASE IV file format).

Exporting charts as files

In some Windows applications such as PageMaker and Word for Windows, you can paste an Excel worksheet graphic from the clipboard. But in other applications (such as Ventura Publisher for the GEM environment), Excel worksheet graphics must be imported as files. In this section, you'll learn how to save charts as Encapsulated Postscript (EPS) files that you can load into most desktop publishing applications.

Before you can save a chart as an EPS file, you must first have the PostScript printer driver installed. For information on installing a printer driver, see the *Windows User's Guide*.

To print a chart to an EPS file, activate the chart you want to print, choose Page Setup from the File menu, and click the Printer Setup button. The Printer Setup dialog box appears. Select a PostScript printer and click the Setup button. The setup dialog box for the printer appears. Click Options. The Options dialog box appears. Select the Encapsulated PostScript File button. Do not type a name. Click OK until you've exited all the dialog boxes. Now you're set up to print an EPS file. Choose Print from the File menu. The Print dialog box appears. Click OK. The Print To File dialog box appears. In the Output File Name text box, type a path and filename for the EPS file and click OK. Now you have an EPS file of the chart for import into a DTP program (such as Ventura Publisher).

To be able to print directly to the PostScript Printer again, choose Page Setup from the File menu, navigate to the Options dialog box again, and select the Printer button. Click OK until you've exited all the dialog boxes.

Exporting Excel worksheet graphics

Some people are more comfortable working with graphics in a drawing application such as CorelDRAW! Here's how to copy a chart to your favorite drawing application: Select the whole chart by choosing Select Chart from the Chart menu, choose Copy from the Edit menu, open the drawing application, and paste the chart on the page (Figure 7-9). Now you can manipulate the chart and save it in any of the drawing application's file formats.

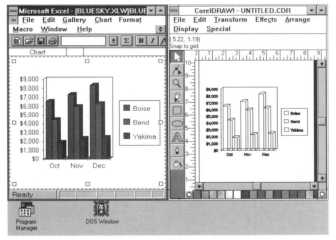

Figure 7-9. *You can copy a chart onto the clipboard, paste it in your favorite drawing application, make changes, and save it in a different file format.*

With multiple worksheets that are based on the same structure and format (such as worksheets based on a template) or worksheets that are dependent on each other (such as linked worksheets), you may find that you want to store them together, arrange them together, or make the same changes to each one. With Excel, it's no big deal. You can assemble worksheets into a single group of documents.

In this section, you'll learn how to handle worksheets, charts, and macro sheets as a group (called *workbooks*).

WORKING WITH MULTIPLE WORKSHEETS

Workbooks let you:

■ Save, open, and close documents as a group.

■ Arrange how the windows appear on the workspace.

Creating workbooks

Before you can use the powerful features of workbooks, you need to create a workbook and add the documents you want to it.

To create a workbook, open *only* the documents (worksheets, macro sheets, or charts) you want to save as a workbook, arrange the document windows in the position and size you want them to be saved, and choose Save Workbook from the File menu. In the File Name text box, type a filename. Click OK. Excel gives workbooks the XLW extension by default.

Now when you save the workbook, Excel saves all the documents in the workbook. When you open the workbook, all the documents will be opened in the position and size you saved them in the workbook.

After you've created a workbook, you'll notice a *workbook contents* window (Figure 7-10). This window lets you manage the documents in a workbook: You can add and remove documents as well as control how each is saved (see the sidebar "The powers that bind").

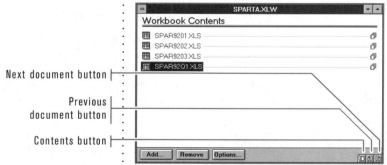

Next document button
Previous document button
Contents button

Figure 7-10. *You can handle worksheets in a workbook through the Workbook Contents window.*

To save a workbook, choose Save Workbook from the File menu.

Handling workbooks

After you've created a workbook, you can add, remove, switch between, and rearrange documents.

To add documents to the workbook, activate the workbook contents window and click the Add button. The Add To Workbook dialog box appears (Figure 7-12). All the currently opened Excel documents appear in the Select Documents To Add list box. To add

The powers that bind

Excel can save the documents contained in a workbook in two ways:

■ Within the workbook file. Excel calls these documents *bound*. The file no longer appears by itself—it's part of the workbook file. By default, documents in a workbook are saved as bound.

■ As separate files linked to the workbook. Excel calls these documents *unbound*. By making a document in a workbook unbound, you can handle that document by itself.

To store a document as unbound, select the document in the Workbook Contents and click the Options button. The Document Options dialog box appears (Figure 7-11). Select the Separate File (Unbound) button and click OK.

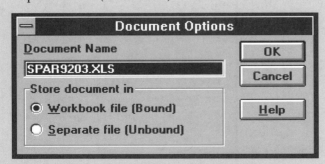

Figure 7-11. *Select how the workbook's documents are saved.*

an open document, select the one you want to add and click Add. To add a document that is not open, click the Open button, use the Open dialog box to open a file, and click OK. When you're finished, click OK to exit the Add To Workbook dialog box.

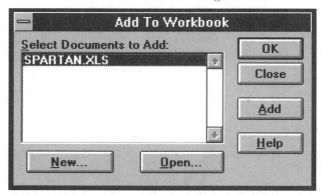

Figure 7-12. *To add a document, select the document and click Add.*

To remove a document from a workbook, select the document in the Workbook Contents window and click the Remove button.

The active document of the workbook has three buttons in the lower-right corner of its window:

■ The contents button (first on the left) switches to the workbook contents within the current window.

■ The previous document button switches to the previous document in the workbook within the current window.

■ The next document button switches to the next document in the workbook within the current window.

To close a workbook and all its documents, choose Close Workbook from the File menu.

To save a new arrangement of the document windows for the workbook, simply use the mouse to resize and position them and choose Save Workbook from the File menu.

EDITING MULTIPLE WORKSHEETS

7

W hen you need to make the same changes to the same cells on multiple worksheets, you can use the Group Edit command to do it fast (Figure 7-13).

To edit worksheets as a group, open all the worksheets to be edited. Then activate the worksheet you'll be changing directly. Choose Group Edit from the Options menu. In the Select Group list box, select the worksheets to edit. Click OK. All those in the edit group now have [Group] in their title bars. Edit the active worksheet (after a command has been completed in the active worksheet, the same command will be executed on other worksheets of the edit group).

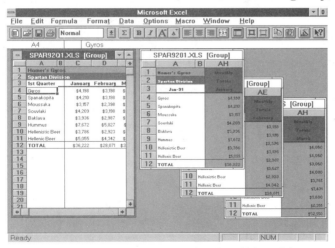

Figure 7-13. *By using Group Edit, you can edit multiple worksheets.*

To stop a group edit session, click another worksheet's window—the session has ended when [Group] is no longer in the active document's title bar.

Unlike a single worksheet, edit groups can only be modified with certain commands — the other commands are grayed out. In addition, there are some commands that are available only to edit groups.

To add or remove worksheets from the edit group, choose Group Edit from the Options menu. Hold down the Shift key and click on the worksheet that you want to remove from the group so that it's no longer highlighted. To add worksheets, hold down the Shift key and click on the worksheet so that it's highlighted. Click OK. The worksheets that are in the edit group are highlighted (Figure 7-14).

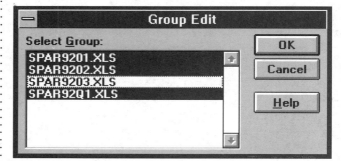

Figure 7-14. *Use the Select Group list box to add and remove worksheets from the edit group.*

In this chapter, you've learned how to link information. In the next chapter, I'll show you how to organize worksheet information into databases and outlines.

CHAPTER 8

ORGANIZING
INFORMATION

It pays to organize your data—because if you can't find it, you can't use it. Excel has two powerful features that make information easy to find, simple to update, and effortless to interpret: databases and outlining.

First, you'll learn how to set up a group of cells as a database within your worksheet. A database lets you handle multiple cells that contain related information as groups (called records). You can find, update, and add records quickly. You'll also find out how to extract records that match any criteria you specify.

You'll also learn how to use the Sort command to sort the database records (or any group of cells).

Finally, you'll learn how to use the outlining feature to set up a hierarchy for your information. You'll assign outline levels to rows and columns. Then you'll be able to collapse or expand the outline to display only the cells at or above a specified outline level—so you can view only the information you need to see.

USING A DATABASE

8

atabases are tools that make it easy for you to access specific information and to reorganize information to suit your needs.

For example, suppose you have a list of beta testers (their names, companies, position, and addresses) for your new word processing software. You could simply type this information directly into an Excel worksheet, but you wouldn't get the advantages of a database (Figure 8-1). For example, Excel lets you find database information that matches a set of criteria (for example, all testers in Seattle) and place that information in a specified group of cells.

But before you try this database feature (I'll explain it at the end of this section), you need to know what databases are and how to create and maintain them.

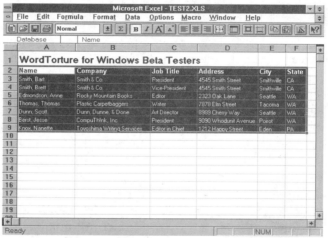

Figure 8-1. *A database is simply information that is organized for easy access.*

Databases are made up of records; records are composed of fields. In Excel, a *record* is a single row of information. All the cells in that row contain data that define that record. For example, in Figure 8-1, row 5 is a record containing information about the beta tester Anne Edmondson. Each record has *fields* that hold a certain characteristic of the record. The names of the fields appear at the top of each column (Name, Company, Job Title, and so on).

A database gives you the advantage of grouping and handling information in larger chunks (records) and using the fields to reorganize (sort) or find (query) the records.

Creating a database

To create a database, you follow two steps:

1. Set up the field names and records.

2. Define the database.

Setting up a database

To set up a database, you start by naming fields. Place the field names in the top row of the database. Use only text for field names—don't use formulas (Figure 8-2).

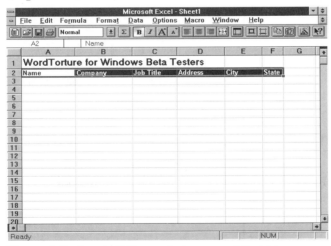

Figure 8-2. *Type the field names in the top row of the database.*

Now, you can enter records into the database as text, numbers, or formulas. Remember that each row is an individual record. You enter the data for the records exactly as you would enter data in any group of worksheet cells. Later, I'll show you an easier way to enter records into a database.

Defining a database

To Excel, the cells you've entered are just like any other group of cells. For Excel to recognize them as a database, you must define that group of cells as a database.

To define a group of cells as a database, select the cells (the field names and all records) and choose Set Database from the Data menu.

Make sure that you leave enough empty cells directly beneath the last record in the database so that more records can be added and the database can expand.

> ### *One defined database per worksheet*
> Excel lets you have only one defined database at a time on a single worksheet. If you have two groups of cells that you've set up as databases on a single worksheet, you must redefine the database to switch from one database to another.

To move to a defined database, choose Goto from the Formula menu, select Database from the Góto list box, and click OK. The cells of a defined database are given the name "Database." So you can move to and select a database just as you would with other named cells.

Entering, modifying, and deleting records

In Excel, you have a powerful database editing tool called the Data Form. It lets you edit records one at a time (Figure 8-3).

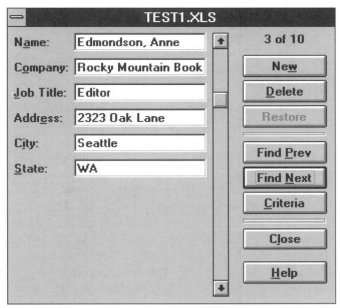

Figure 8-3. *The Data Form dialog box for our example database.*

To use the Data Form, choose Form from the Data menu. The Data Form dialog box appears (Figure 8-3). The worksheet's filename appears in the Data Form's title bar.

Using the Data Form is the simplest way to enter new records, delete records, edit existing records, and find records. Here's how:

■ To navigate from record to record, you can use the scroll bar to move through the database. In the next section, I'll show you an easier way to find records.

■ To enter a new record, click the New button, and enter the text or numbers for the record. To add the record to the database and add another new record, click New. To add the record and exit the Data Form, click Close.

■ To delete a record, navigate to the record using the scroll box and click the Delete button.

■ To edit a record, navigate to the record and edit the text or numbers in the field text boxes. To carry out the changes, navigate to another record or click

Close. If you want to revert to the previous version of the record, click Restore.

> ### *How many records are in the database?*
> The Data Form also displays the total number of records in the database and the record number of the currently displayed record in the upper right corner of the dialog box.

Finding records

To find a database record, move the scroll box to the top of the scroll bar and click Criteria. Type the information (criteria) you want to use to find a database record in the field text boxes. Click Find Next. The first record that has data that matches the criteria you specified should appear. If Excel can't find a match, you'll hear a beep.

To find the next matching record, click Find Next. To find the previous matching record, click Find Previous.

Sorting records

Records are rarely entered into a database in the order you want them organized. For example, customer and sales records are often entered by date or by purchase. However, you usually want to sort customer records according to customer name. Excel lets you sort records alphabetically and numerically. The fields that are used to sort the database records are called *keys*. The first key is the first field that Excel uses to sort the database. If the first key has records that have identical field entries (for example, two people named Smith), you can specify a second key or third key to sort those records (John Smith's record would be placed ahead of Paul Smith's).

To sort the database records, select the records you want to sort. Make sure that the field names are not selected (if you select the field names at the top of the database, they will be sorted with the rest of the records). Choose Sort from the Data menu. The Sort dialog box appears (Figure 8-4). From the Sort By buttons, select Rows to sort the database's fields by rows (records). In the 1st Key text box, type the cell reference for the cell you want to use as the first key. Select Ascending (sorts from A to Z) or Descending (sorts from Z to A) to specify the direction of the sort. You can also specify second and third keys. Click OK.

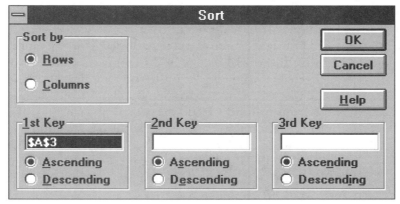

Figure 8-4. *You can sort selected cells by row or by column with the Data Sort command.*

> ### *Sorting selected cells*
> The Sort command isn't restricted to databases—you can also use it to sort any group of cells by row or column using the same procedure. Just select the cells and use the Sort command from the Data menu.

Extracting database information

Now that you know how to get data into a database, here's how to get the data you want out.

You can find the records that have fields containing the specific data you want. The records that contain the data can be copied (called *extracting*) to a group of cells called the *extract range*. In fact, you can specify which fields of the matching records get extracted.

Before you try extracting, you must have a defined database.

To extract records from a database, you follow three steps:

1. Define the criteria to use to find the records you want.

2. Define the cells where you want to extract the records.

3. Extract the data.

Defining the extraction criteria

To define extraction criteria, find a group of empty cells on the worksheet (you'll need two rows but not necessarily whole rows). In the top row, type the field name where you want to match the data (for example, City if you wanted to find records that match a city). In the row below, type the text, value, or formula you want to match (for example, an actual city name such as Seattle). The field name and specific entry you want to match make up the *extraction criteria*, which Excel uses to find the matching records. If you want to narrow the criteria further (for example, all Smiths in Seattle), you can add as many fields and desired entries as you want. When you've entered all the extraction criteria, select the cells containing the criteria, and choose Set Criteria from the Data menu. This defines extraction criteria (Figure 8-5).

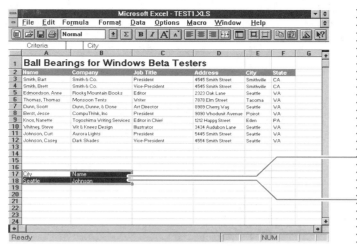

Type the field names
in the first row.

Type the data you
want to find in the
second row.

Figure 8-5. *Defining the extraction criteria.*

Defining the extract area

To define the cells where you'll extract the records, find a group of empty cells (make sure there are enough rows for all the records you want to extract and enough columns for all the fields you want to show). In the top row, type the names of the fields for which you want to see data. (For example, if you want to show only the Name and Job Title from the record, type only those field names in the top row. If you want to see all the fields, type all the field names.) Then select the field names you've typed and enough cells directly below them so that all the records that you want to extract can fit. Choose Set Extract from the Data menu. This defines the extract area (Figure 8-7).

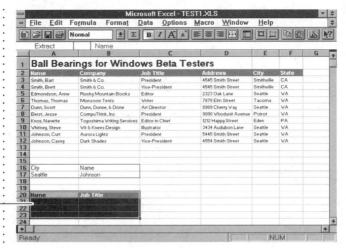

Figure 8-7. *Defining the extract area.*

Extracting the data

To extract the record information, choose Extract from the Data menu and click OK. The data is extracted from the database and placed in the extract area (Figure 8-6).

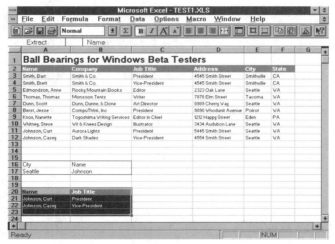

Figure 8-6. *Extracting the data.*

USING AN OUTLINE

An outline lets you display different levels of worksheet information. Just as you can collapse and expand heading levels in a word processor like

Microsoft Word, you can collapse and expand the rows and columns in Excel.

To create an outline, all you do is assign outline levels to rows and columns. Then you can collapse or expand the outline to display only cells at or above a specified outline level, and hide all other cells.

In this section, you'll learn the basics of outlines:

■ How to use the outline tools.

■ How to assign outline levels to rows and columns.

■ How to display the outline levels you want to see and hide the ones you don't.

■ How to select cells in an outline.

Using the outline tools

Before you start outlining, you need the right tools.

To access the outline tools, choose Toolbars from the Options menu, select Utility from the Show Toolbars menu, and click OK (Figure 8-8).

Outline tools

Figure 8-8. *Display the Utility toolbar so you can use the outline tools.*

If you handle outlines a lot, you may want to add the outline tools to your custom toolbar. Otherwise, you can just display the Utility toolbar when you need those tools.

Here's the rundown on the four outline tools:

The **Demote tool** moves the selected row or column down one outline level.

The **Promote tool** moves the selected row or column up one outline level.

The **Show Outline Symbols tool** shows or hides the outline display. If the worksheet doesn't have an outline, Excel makes one for you.

The **Select Visible Cells tool** selects only the cells you see in a collapsed outline–without affecting the cells in levels that have been collapsed (hidden).

Assigning outline levels

The easiest way is to use the Demote tool.

To assign an outline level to a row or column, select the row or column and press the Demote button on the Utility toolbar (the arrow that points to the right). This assigns outline level 1 (the topmost level) to the selected row or column. To assign lower levels, click the Demote button until you have the level you want. The row buttons and column buttons show the levels that have been applied (Figure 8-9).

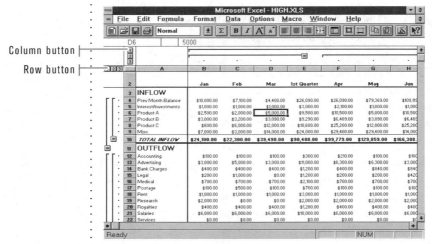

Figure 8-9. *Outlines let you display and hide rows and columns. This outline is completely expanded.*

Note that rows and columns that are *not* assigned outline levels will always be displayed.

To assign higher levels, select the row or column and click the Promote tool until you have the level you want.

To clear all outline settings, expand the outline, select all rows and columns that have been assigned outline levels, and click the Promote button until the row buttons and column buttons disappear.

Displaying outline levels

To display a specific outline level and those above it, click on the appropriate row button or column button (Figure 8-10):

■ To display all levels in rows or columns, click the lowest-level row button or column button.

■ To expand the levels below a specific outlined row or column, click its expand button (the button with a plus sign).

■ To collapse the levels below a specific outlined row or column, click its collapse button (the button with a minus sign).

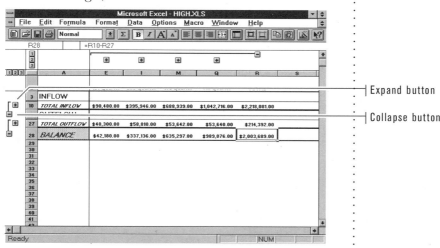

Figure 8-10. *This is a collapsed outline.*

And of course, the Show Outline Symbols tool lets you display or hide outline symbols on your worksheet.

Selecting outlined cells

By default, when you select a range of cells in a collapsed level, you also select the cells directly below it.
To select only the visible cells in a collapsed outline,
select the cells and click the Select Visible Cells tool.

You've learned almost all the basics you need to get
up and running. In the last chapter, I'll cover
macros, a feature that saves time by automating
repeated tasks.

CHAPTER 9

SPEEDING UP WITH MACROS

So far, you've learned the basic skills for getting the end results you want—from creating worksheets to making charts to printing it all out. But if you're like me, you're always wondering if there's an easier and faster way to do things. If there's a task, a set of commands, or a calculation that you do again and again, you'd probably like to repeat them with simply a press of a button.

Excel lets you create macros that save you from the tedium of doing the same tasks repeatedly and help you prevent typing errors. *Macros* are just a way to store Excel actions, commands, and functions so that you can reuse them in any way you want.

A macro can be as simple as recording a sequence of commands and then "playing" them back to repeat those commands. In this chapter, you'll learn the simplest technique: Recording macros with Excel's macro recorder and then playing them back.

This chapter doesn't tell everything about macros—it's just a taste to get you started.

9 RECORDING MACROS

Using Excel's macro recorder is a lot like using a tape recorder. With a tape recorder, you simply put in a tape, turn on the recorder, and start talking. When you're done, you shut it off. Then you can rewind it and play it back. If you've got the sophisticated equipment, you can even edit your tape.

Excel's macro recorder does the same thing for actions that happen in Excel. When you turn on the recorder, Excel records every action you make in Excel. After you turn off the recorder, you can repeat those same actions again by running the macro.

Just as a tape recorder records sounds on tape, Excel stores macros on a macro sheet. To run a macro, you need to open the macro sheet that contains the desired macro—just as you would need the right tape to play your favorite song. You can also edit macros (thereby changing how they run) directly on the macro sheet. In fact, you can create new macros by entering them directly into the cells of the macro sheet.

In this section, you'll learn how to use the macro recorder. Later, you'll learn how to run macros and assign them to key combinations or toolbar tools.

Starting the recorder

To start recording a macro, choose Record from the Macro menu. The Record Macro text box appears (Figure 9-1). In the Name text box, type a name for the macro. In the Key text box, type a Ctrl key shortcut (a single keyboard character). From the Store Macro In buttons, select whether to store the macro on the global macro sheet or an open macro sheet. (For more information about where macros are recorded, see the sidebar "Where macros are recorded.") Click OK to begin recording.

From this point, every action within Excel will be recorded. Do the actions that you want recorded. When you're done, choose Stop Recorder from the Macro menu.

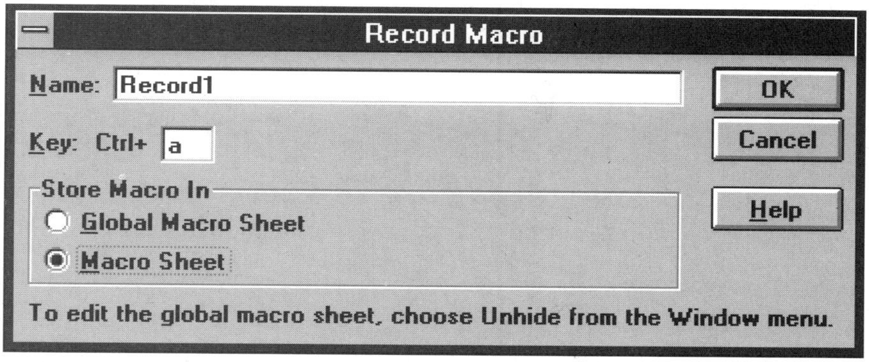
Record Macro
Name: Record1
Key: Ctrl+ a
Store Macro In
Global Macro Sheet
Macro Sheet
OK
Cancel
Help
To edit the global macro sheet, choose Unhide from the Window menu.

Figure 9-1. *Give your macro a name and assign it a shortcut key.*

You can use the defaults for the macro name and key combination. The Name text box contains a suggested name for the macro ("Record*number*", for example "Record1"). The Key text box contains an available Ctrl key combination (such as Ctrl-a).

To pause the recording, choose Stop Recorder from the Macro menu. Note that the pause and anything occurring during the pause are not recorded.

To continue recording, choose Start Recorder from the Macro menu.

Saving macros

After you record the macro, make sure you save the macro sheet you've stored it on. To save the macro sheet, activate its window, choose Save from the File menu, navigate to the directory where you want to store it with the Directories box, type a filename in the File Name text box, and click OK. Excel gives macro sheets the XLM extension by default.

Running and Assigning Macros

After you've created your macros, Excel gives you lots of ways to run them. There are two simple ways:

- Use the Run command from the Macro menu.
- Assign the macro to a key combination or toolbar tool. After the macro has been assigned, you can

9

start the macro by pressing the key combination or clicking on the tool.

Which method should you use? The key is making it as painless as possible. Here are some tips:

■ *Use the Run command when testing macros.* If you've just written or recorded a macro, you won't want to go to the trouble of assigning it to a tool before you're sure it does exactly what you want. Just run it with the Run command.

■ *Use the Run command for macros that you don't use very often.* You'll avoid the clutter of extra tools on your toolbar and you won't unintentionally run macros

Where macros are recorded

You need to know a little more about where Excel stores your macro so you know where to find it. You can store the macro on the *global macro sheet*, which is opened (but usually hidden) each time you start Excel. Or you can store it on an open macro sheet. If no macro sheet is open, a new macro sheet will be created.

Here's the advantages of each type:

■ Macros on the global macro sheet are available when you first start Excel. Global macros are a good place to store macros you use with any worksheet.

■ Macros on a regular macro sheet are easily accessible if the macro sheet is opened. If it's not open, you need to make an explicit reference to the macro sheet—it's easier just to open the macro sheet. A regular macro sheet can be handy if you want macros to be available only with certain worksheets—but not others. You can simplify things by combining the worksheets and macro sheet together in a workbook.

with a forgotten key combination. Plus, you'll keep key combinations free for the macros you use most often.

- *Use key combinations for macros used while typing.* If you have a macro you use while typing (for example, a macro to insert a complex series of functions when you're typing a formula), use a key combination so you can get to the macro without having to move from the keyboard to the mouse and back again.

- *Assign the macro to a tool for quick access.* If you have a macro that does a complex calculation or action and you use it a lot, assign it to a tool. Then you can simply click the tool to run the macro.

Using the Run command

To run any macro, you must either have the macro sheet on which it's located open or make an explicit reference to that macro. The simplest way is to open the macro sheet. But if you want to conserve memory, make an explicit reference.

To run a macro with the macro sheet already open, activate the worksheet upon which you want the macro to act. If the macro acts on a selected cell or group of cells, make sure that those cells are selected. Choose Run from the Macro menu. The Run dialog box appears (Figure 9-2). The Run list box displays all the defined macros from all the open macro sheets. From the Run list box, select the macro. Click OK.

9

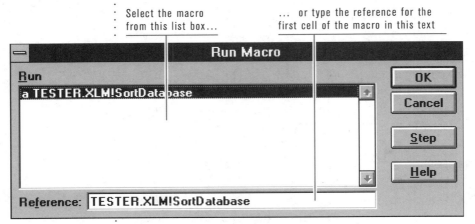

Select the macro from this list box...

... or type the reference for the first cell of the macro in this text

Run Macro

R̲un

a TESTER.XLM!SortDatabase

OK

Cancel

S̲tep

H̲elp

R̲eference: | TESTER.XLM!SortDatabase |

Figure 9-2. *Select a macro from an open macro sheet.*

To run a macro with an explicit reference, activate the worksheet where you want to run the macro and choose Run from the Macro menu. The Run Macro dialog box appears. In the Reference text box, type the reference for the macro's first cell on the macro sheet. Click OK.

Recall that references have the form:

$$'drive:\backslash path \backslash filename'!cell$$
$$reference.$$

Running a macro one step at a time

When you record a macro, Excel puts each command it records in an individual cell in the macro sheet. You can run a macro one cell at a time (*step* through the macro). If you're trying to find where a macro fails or doesn't do what you want, you can use the step feature to find where the problem occurs and edit the macro.

To step through a macro with the macro sheet already open, activate the worksheet upon which you want the macro to act. If the macro acts on a selected cell or group of cells, make sure that those cells are selected. Choose Run from the Macro menu. From the Run list box, select the macro. Click Step. The Single Step dialog box appears (Figure 9-3). The cell about to be run on the macro sheet is displayed beneath the Formula: line.

To carry out the current macro cell and go to the next one, click Step Into.

To skip the the current macro cell, click Step Over.

To stop the macro, click Halt.

To make the macro continue running to completion without stepping, click Continue.

To pause the macro, click Pause.

To see the value (if applicable) that the macro cell evaluates to, click Evaluate. The value appears beneath the Formula: line.

To stop the macro and go to the macro sheet and the cell where the macro stopped, click Goto.

Figure 9-3. *Use this dialog box to step through the macro one cell at a time.*

Stopping a macro

To stop a macro while it's running, press the Esc key. A message box appears and tells you which macro has been stopped and at which cell it has stopped within the macro sheet (Figure 9-5). To terminate the macro at that point, click Halt. To continue running the macro, click Continue. To terminate the macro and go to the macro sheet and cell where the macro stopped, press Goto. To step through the macro, click Step.

9

Editing macros

Suppose you used the recorder to create a long macro—but you made one small error, such as not selecting all the records in a database. You don't have to re-record the macro.

You can simply open the macro sheet containing the macro and edit the macro code yourself. You already know how to handle formulas. Each cell of a macro is simply a formula. A macro is a column of cells on a macro sheet. When you run a macro, each cell is carried out one after another.

After recording the macro, Excel has done most of the hard work for you, that is, finding the functions that correspond to the actions you want to carry out. Usually, you just need to change the arguments used by the macro functions.

You can also add conditional functions to control the flow of the macro such as IF() or loop functions to repeat actions such as WHILE() and NEXT(). Figure 9-4 shows a macro with a loop to repeat the actions within the loop. These are just some of the "programming" possiblities you have with Excel macros.

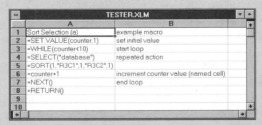

Figure 9-4. *By using a loop in your macro, you can repeat actions as many times as you like (9 times, in this case).*

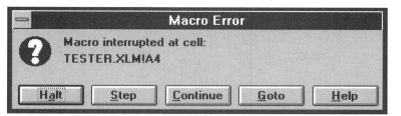

Figure 9-5. *Press the Esc key to suspend a macro and use this dialog box to control the macro's execution.*

Assigning macros to key combinations

You can start a macro by pressing a combination of keys (the Ctrl key and a letter key). All you have to do is assign the key combination to the macro. This can be done when you first record the macro.

To change the key combination, activate the macro sheet containing the macro, choose Define Name from the Formula menu (Figure 9-6) and select the macro from the Names In Sheet list box. In the Key: Ctrl+ entry box, type a letter you want to use for the key combination. Click OK.

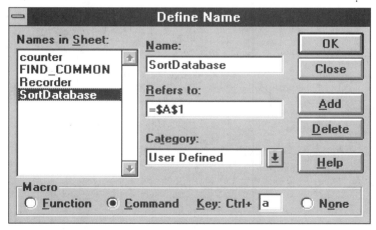

Figure 9-6. *To change a key combination, select the macro and type a letter in the Key: Ctrl+ entry box.*

9

Assigning macros to toolbar tools

The toolbar is an easy way to get to Excel's most common commands. But that's not all. You can also assign macros to tools so that you can run your macros from the toolbar.

To add a macro to a tool on the toolbar, open the toolbar to which you want to add the macro, click the toolbar with the right mouse button, and choose Custom from the shortcut menu. In the Categories list box, select Custom. The available tools (ones that don't already have an Excel command assigned to them) appear in the Tools box (Figure 9-7). Drag the desired tool button to the toolbar you want to add it to. The Assign To Tool dialog box appears (Figure 9-8). In the Assign Macro list box, select the macro to assign to the tool. Click OK. Then click Close.

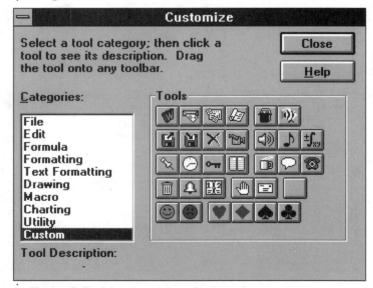

Figure 9-7. *Select the tool to use for the macro.*

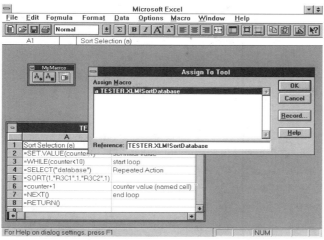

Figure 9-8. *Select the macro to assign to the tool.*

To make a macro sheet open when you start Excel...

...place the macro sheet in the \XLSTART subdirectory of the directory where Excel is installed. Usually, this is the C:\EXCEL\XLSTART directory. In fact, any Excel file (workspaces, worksheets, macro sheets, and charts) placed in the \XLSTART subdirectory is opened automatically.

You now know the essential parts of Excel. You've learned how to create the basic types of Excel documents (worksheets, charts, and macro sheets) and get some practical use out of them quickly. Now, you've got the skill to explore Excel's many features on your own.

9

Toolbar Tips

Add these handy tools to your toolbar to make working with macros a snap:

The **Record Macro tool** lets you start recording a macro. This tool opens the Record Macro dialog box just like the Record command from the Macro menu.

The **Stop Recording tool** stops recording a macro.

The **Run Macro tool** runs a macro. This tool opens the Run Macro dialog box just like the Run command from the Macro menu.

The **Step Macro tool** lets you run a macro by going through it one macro cell at a time. This tool opens the Single Step dialog box just like the Step button in the Run Macro dialog box.

The **Resume Macro tool** restarts a macro after it has been paused.

INDEX

A

active cell, 4
  creating, 12
  illustrated, 4
adding
  cell entry characters, 48
  chart text, 94-95
  worksheets to edit group,
    138
alignment, 58-59
  options, 59-60
  setting page, 117-118
Alignment tools, 7, 77
ampersand (&), 114-115
application window, 3
  illustrated, 4
arguments, 40
  multiple, 43
  See also functions
Arrow tool, 99
AutoFormat, 71
  using, 72-73
AutoFormat tool, 7
  for predefined table
    formats, 8
AutoSum tool, 6
  for summing range of
    cells, 8
AVERAGE function, 40
axis scale, 96

B

Bold tool, 6, 77
borders
  color of, 64
  formatting, 63-65
  removing, 64
Bottom Border tool, 7

C

callouts, 103, 104
Camera tool, 104-105
cancel button, 5
capturing screen pictures,
  104-105
categories, 82
  grouping graphs in, 93
cell borders, 63-65
cell patterns, 65-66
cell reference, 2
cells, 2
  active, 4, 12
  aligning, 58-61
  contents
    editing, 48
    moving/copying, 49-50
  copying, 9, 49
    selected characteristics
      of, 49
  defining group of, 142
  deleting, 51
  extending selection of, 13
  finding, 69
    referenced, 71
  formatting, 8
  inserting, 52
  linked copy of, 122-127
  long entries in, 25-28
  moving, 9, 49
    automatically, 37

pointing to, 44
ranges of, 12
    colon in, 43
    naming, 14-15
    removing name from, 15
resizing, 29
rotating, 58-61
selecting, 12-13
    all, 13
    to chart, 82
    groups of, 12-13
    noncontinuous ranges of, 13
    outlined, 152
    to print, 109
shortcuts for referring to, 43-46
sorting, 145
summing, 19
    range of, 8
text in, 25-28
    fitting, 29-31
See also references
cell styles, 71
    using, 71-72
Center Across Columns tool, 7
characters
    finding, 66-69
    replacing, 69
Charting toolbar, 99
Chart menu, 91
    Attach Text command, 94
    Select Chart command, 90, 133
charts, 3
    3-D line, 83
    adding legend, title, axis labels to, 88
    axis scale, 96
    column, 93-94
    creating, 9, 80-100
        five-steps for, 85-88
    editing, 9, 91-97
    embedded, 89
    exporting, 132-133
    formats for, 86
    formatting elements of, 95-96
    formatting text for, 95
    generating, 84
    line, 93

opening in document window, 91
pie, 92-93
placing data in, 87
printing to EPS file, 132
rotating 3-D, 97-98
saving, 89
selecting data for, 82
sizing, 89, 116-117
templates for, 90-91
    creating, 90
    embedding, 90
    filenames for, 91
    using, 90
terminology, 80-82
tips on making, 83
tools for, 98-100
types of, 91-92
    changing, 94
    cycling through, 94
using in other applications, 96
See also ChartWizard
Chart Size buttons, 117
ChartWizard
    dialog boxes, 85-88
        fifth, 88
        first, 85
        fourth, 87
        second, 85
        third, 86
    tool, 7, 84, 85, 99
        for creating charts, 9, 85-88
    using, 84-89
    See also charts
Check Spelling tool, 76
Clear Formats tool, 76
Clear Formulas tool, 76
codes, header/footer, 114-115
colon (:), 55
column charts, 93
    illustrated, 94
columns, 2
    controlling width of, 65
    hiding headings for, 116
    inserting, 52
    number of, 5
    outlines and, 150-151
    resizing, 29
        shortcut, 30
    selecting, 13
    titles for, 30-31

freezing, 31
repeating, 118-119
rotating, 60
See also rows
commas (,), 55
constants, 2
copying
    cells, 9, 49
        selected characteristics
            of, 49
    formulas/values from
        above cell, 37
    See also moving
Copy tool, 7
CoreIDRAW, 129, 133
creating
    charts, 9, 80-100
        five steps for, 85-88
    chart templates, 90-91
    custom date and time
        formats, 55-56
    custom number formats,
        54-58
    custom toolbars, 20-21
    databases, 141-142
    footers, 113-116
    formulas with linked
        references, 128-129
    headers, 113-116
    linked copy of cells,
        122-127
    outlines, 149
    row and column titles,
        30-31
    templates, 73-75
    workbooks, 134
currency, entering, 32
Currency Style tool, 78

D

data
    exporting, as files, 131-132
    extracting, 148
    marker, 80, 81
    selecting, for chart, 82
    series, 81
        names for, 82
    using, in other
        applications, 130
databases, 140-141
    advantages, 141
    creating, 141-142

defining, 142
setting up, 141
using, 140-148
See also fields; records
Data Form editing tool, 142
    using, 143
Data menu, 35
    Extract command, 148
    Form command, 143
    Set Criteria command, 146
    Set Database command,
        142
    Set Extract command, 147
    Sort command, 145
dates
    changing display of, 9
    entering, 33
        current, 37
        series of, 9
    Excel storage of, 34
    formats for, 55-56
    restoring formats for, 54
    See also times
date unit, 36
decimal, fixed entry, 36-37
Decimal tools, 78
Decrease Font Size tool, 6
deleting
    cells, 51
        avoiding accidental, 6-7
    entry characters, 48
    graphics, 101
    page breaks, 120
    records, 143
Demote tool, 149
    for assigning outline
        levels, 150
destination worksheets,
    122-123, 124
    linking to, 130
    See also workbooks;
        worksheets
dialog boxes, list of
    Add to Workbook, 135,
        136
    Alignment, 58
    Assign To Tool, 162
    Attach Text To, 94-95
    Border, 64
    Change Links, 125
    Clear, 126
    Customize, 20
    Data Form, 143
    Define Name, 15

Delete, 51
Document Options, 135
Find, 67
Font, 8, 61, 115
Footer, 113
Header, 113
Insert, 52
Links, 125
Number Format, 9, 53, 54
Open, 136
Options, 132
Page Setup, 108, 111, 113, 116
Paste Special, 127
Patterns, 65, 102-103
Print, 132
Printer Setup, 108, 109
Replace, 69
Run, 157
Run Macro, 158
Save As, 131
Scale, 97
Select Special, 70
Series, 36
Set Print Titles, 119
Single Step, 158
Sort, 145
Toolbars, 19
documents
    bound, 135
    putting back in window, 137
    workbook, 135-136
    See also files
document windows, 3
    illustrated, 4
    opening charts in, 91
dollar signs ($), 45
drawing
    graphics, 100-101
    perfect, 101
Drawing toolbar, 100
Dynamic Data Exchange (DDE), 130

E

editing
    cell contents, 48
    charts, 9, 91-97
    fast, 52
    group, 137-138
    macros, 160

multiple worksheets, 137-138
    records, 143
    tools, 76
Edit menu
    Clear command, 126
    Copy command, 50, 90, 101, 127, 130
    Cut command, 101
    Delete command, 51
    Insert command, 52
    Paste command, 90, 101, 130
    Paste Link command, 122, 130
    Paste Special command, 49, 50, 127
    Redo command, 52
    Undo command, 52
Encapsulated Postscript (EPS) files, 132
enter button, 5
entering
    formulas, 8, 37-46
    numbers, 8, 32-37
    records, 143
    series, 33-36
    text, 8, 24-31, 36-37
        steps for, 24-25
entry
    area, 4
    cell, editing, 48
equal sign, in formulas, 42
exporting
    charts as files, 132-133
    data as files, 131-132
    Excel worksheet graphics, 133
extracting, 145
    data, 148
    database information, 145-148
extraction criteria, 146-147
extract range, 145

F

fields, 140-141
    keys, 144
    naming, 141
    See also databases
File menu, 26
    for backup files, 27

Close Workbook
   command, 136
Exit command, 74
New command, 74, 90
Open command, 74, 75
Page Setup command,
   108, 112, 132
Print command, 120, 132
Print Preview command,
   109, 112
Save As command, 74,
   124, 131
Save command, 89, 90
Save Workbook
   command, 134, 136
files
   backup, 27
   EPS, 132
   exporting charts as,
      132-133
   exporting data as, 131-132
   extensions for, 131-132
   formats for, 131
   names of, 26-27
   setting up, 26-27
   See also documents
finding
   characters/numbers,
      66-69
   fast, 69
   options, 68
   records, 144
   referenced cells, 71
   specific contents, 70-71
   switching directions and,
      69
fonts
   changing settings, 8
   choosing, 63
   do's and dont's, 62
   formatting, 63
      header/footer, 115
   Printer, 61-62
   Screen, 63
   setting, 61-63
   TrueType, 63
Font tool, 115
footers, 113-116
   avoiding overlapping of,
      115
   codes, 114-115
Format menu, 91
   AutoFormat command, 72
   Patterns command, 65

scientific notation and, 32
Send to Back command,
   104
Send to Front command,
   104
formats
   date
      custom, 55-56
      restoring, 54
   file, 131
   number, 54-58
      adding symbols to, 57
      adding text to, 57
      sequence of, 57
   time, 55-56
formatting
   alignment, 58
   cell, 8
      borders, 63-65
      patterns, 65-66
   chart elements, 95-96
   chart text, 95
   fast, 71-75
   fonts, 63
   lines, 102-103
   numbers, 52-54
   shapes, 103
   tools, 77-78
   worksheets, 52-66
formula bar, 4
   activating, 4
   cell contents and, 25-28
   illustrated, 4
   typing formulas and, 39
Formula menu, 14-15
   Apply Names command,
      46
   Define Name command,
      161
   Find command, 66, 67
   Goto command, 142
   Paste Function command,
      40, 41
   Replace command, 66, 69
formulas, 2-3
   adjusting, 50
   copying from above cell,
      37
   creating, 41-43
      using linked
         references, 128-129
   defined, 38
   entering, 8, 37-46
   equal sign and, 42

INDEX

evaluating, 37
operation order in, 42-43
parenthesis and, 43
quotation marks and, 43
references in, 43
typing, 38-39
fractions, entering, 32
freezing, row and column
  titles, 31
functions
  built-in, 39
  entering manually, 41
  list of important, 42
  in macros, 160
  Paste Function tool and,
    46
  selecting, 40
  using, 39-41
  See also arguments

G

Gallery menu, 91, 94
GEM environment, 132
graphics
  changing stacking order
    of, 104
  combining, 104
  drawing, 100-101
  exporting, 133
  multiple worksheet,
    103-104
  sizing, moving, deleting,
    101
graphs (data markers), 81
  illustrated, 80
gridlines, hiding, 116
groups, editing, 137-138
  adding/removing
    worksheets from, 138

H

headers, 113-116
  avoiding overlapping of,
    115
  codes, 114-115
headings, 2
  hiding, 116
  rotating, 60
  See also titles
Help tool, 7

Horizontal Gridlines tool, 99
hyphens (-), 55

I

Increase Font Size tool, 6, 77
inserting
  cells, 52
  line breaks, 29
  rows and columns, 52
insertion point, 4-5
Italic tool, 6, 77

K

keyboard, 3
keyboard shortcuts
  Alt-F-S, 26
  Ctrl+1, 63
  Ctrl+2, 63
  Ctrl+3, 63
  Ctrl-,' 37
  Ctrl-Insert, 49
  Ctrl-Shift-," 37
key combinations, 157
  assigning macros to, 161
keys, 144

L

layout
  diagonal, 6-7
    illustrated, 10
  page, 110
    setting up, 111-113
legend, 82
  adding, 88
Legend tool, 99
levels, outline
  assigning, 150-151
  displaying, 151
line breaks, 115
  inserting, 29
  manual, 115
line charts, 93
lines, formatting, 102-103
linking
  to other applications,
    129-133
  rules for, 124

to Window applications,
129-131
links
backtracking through, 123
controlling, 123-127
redirecting, 125
severing, 126-127
delete destination
values and, 126
keep destination
values and, 127
ways to create, 121
list boxes, list of
Assign Macro, 162
Category, 34, 53, 162
Color, 64, 103
Directories, 125
Directory, 27
File Name, 27
Font, 62
Format Codes, 53
Function Category, 41
Goto, 142
Group Edit, 137
Links, 125
Names In Sheet, 161
New, 90
Operation, 50
Paper, 118
Paste Function, 40-41
Pattern, 66
Printer, 108
Run, 157
Save File As Type, 74, 90,
131
Selected Documents To
Add, 135
Show Toolbars, 19
Styles, 71, 103
Table Format, 72
Weight, 103
logos, 103

M

Macro menu
Record command, 154,
155
Run command, 155-156,
158
using, 157-158
Stop Record command,
154, 155

macros, 153
assigning
to key combinations,
161
to toolbar tools,
162-163
editing, 160
functions in, 160
key combinations for, 157
loops within, 160
recording, 154-155
running, 157-159
saving, 155
stepping through, 158
stopping, 159
storing, 156
testing, 156
macro sheets, 3, 154
global, 156
open when starting Excel,
163
saving, 155
See also macros
margins, setting, 112-113
menu bar, 4
illustrated, 4
menus
See specific types of menus
mouse, 3
moving and copying cells
with, 49
moving
cells, 9, 49
graphics, 101
within worksheets, 14-15
See also copying

N

New Worksheet tool, 6
numbers
cell alignment of, 58
changing display of, 9
displaying negative, 54
entering, 8, 32-37
currency, 32
dates, 33
exponential notation,
32
fast, 36-37
fractions, 32
negative, 32
percentages, 32

positive, 32
series of, 9
times, 33
finding, 66-69
formatting, 52-54
starting page, 116
suppressing, 58

O

Open File tool, 6
opening, existing
  worksheets, 27
operations, performance
  order of, 42
operators, 38
  level of precedence of, 43
Options menu, 19, 20
  for fixed decimal entry, 37
  Group Edit command,
    137, 138
  for moving to cells
    automatically, 37
  Remove Page Break
    command, 120
  Remove Print Area
    command, 109
  Remove Print Titles
    command, 119
  Set Page Break command,
    119
  Set Print Area command,
    109
  Set Print Titles command,
    118
  Toolbars command, 149
orientation
  See alignment
Orientation tools, 77
Outline Border tool, 7
outlines
  clearing settings for, 151
  collapsed, 152
  creating, 149
  function of, 148-149
  levels of
    assigning, 150-151
    displaying, 151
  tools for, 149-150
Oval tool, 100, 101

P

page
  boundaries, 118
  breaks, 119-120
    removing, 120
  layout, 110
    setting up, 111-113
  numbers, starting, 116
  orientation, 117-118
  sequence, 118
  size, 117-118
  titles on every, 118-119
PageMaker, 132
paper size, 118
parenthesis, in formulas, 43
Paste Formats tool, 7, 76
Paste Function tool, 46
Paste Values tool, 76
percentages, entering, 32
Percent Style tool, 78
pie charts, 92
  illustrated, 93
pound sign (#), 53, 55, 56-57
Preferred Chart tool, 99
printer
  PostScript, 13, 117, 118
  selecting, 108-109
Printer fonts, 61-62
printing, 9, 107-120
  documents, 120
  to EPS file, 132
Print Preview mode, 110
  for page layout, 110,
    111-118
  switching to, 109-111
Print Preview tool, 120
Print tool, 6, 120
Promote tool, 149
  in assigning outline levels,
    151

Q

question mark (?), 53, 55,
  56-57
quotation marks, in
  formulas, 43

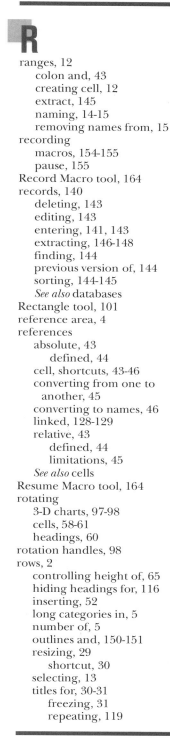

R

ranges, 12
  colon and, 43
  creating cell, 12
  extract, 145
  naming, 14-15
  removing names from, 15
recording
  macros, 154-155
  pause, 155
Record Macro tool, 164
records, 140
  deleting, 143
  editing, 143
  entering, 141, 143
  extracting, 146-148
  finding, 144
  previous version of, 144
  sorting, 144-145
  See also databases
Rectangle tool, 101
reference area, 4
references
  absolute, 43
    defined, 44
  cell, shortcuts, 43-46
  converting from one to
    another, 45
  converting to names, 46
  linked, 128-129
  relative, 43
    defined, 44
    limitations, 45
  See also cells
Resume Macro tool, 164
rotating
  3-D charts, 97-98
  cells, 58-61
  headings, 60
rotation handles, 98
rows, 2
  controlling height of, 65
  hiding headings for, 116
  inserting, 52
  long categories in, 5
  number of, 5
  outlines and, 150-151
  resizing, 29
    shortcut, 30
  selecting, 13
  titles for, 30-31
    freezing, 31
    repeating, 119

  See also columns
Run Macro tool, 164

S

Save File tool, 6
saving
  charts, 89
  macros, 155
  workbooks, 134
  worksheets, 26
scientific notation, entering,
  32
Screen fonts, 63
scroll bars, 14
  for moving within
    worksheet, 14
searching
  See finding
Select All button, 5
  illustrated, 4
Select Visible Cells tool, 150,
  152
series
  entering, 33-36
    complex, 35-36
  growth, 36
  linear, 36
Set Print Area tool, 120
Shift-Enter, 115
shortcut menu, 18
  for adding toolbars, 20
  Alignment command, 58
  Border command, 64
  Copy command, 122
  Custom command, 162
  Number command, 52-53,
    54
Show Outline Symbols tool,
  150, 151
Show Toolbars menu, 149
sizing
  charts, 116-117
  column widths, 113
  graphics, 101
  picture, 105
  worksheets, 116
slashes (/), 55
sorting
  records, 144-145
  selected cells, 145
source worksheets, 122-123,
  124

INDEX

linking to, 130
See also workbooks;
worksheets
spaces, 55
SQRT function, 40
Standard toolbar, 4
ChartWizard and, 84
illustrated, 6
See also toolbars
status bar, 5
illustrated, 4
Step Macro tool, 164
step value, 35
in complex series, 35-36
Stop Recording tool, 164
stop value, 36
Style box, 6
styles, cell, 71-72
See also fonts
SUM formula, 43
summing, group of cells, 19

T

templates, 71
changes to, 75
chart, 90-91
filenames for, 91
creating, 73-75
See also worksheets
text
alignment, 58
chart, 94-95
in custom number
formats, 57
entering, 8, 24-31
fast, 36-37
steps for, 24-25
long, in cells, 25-28
replacing, 69-70
unattached, 95
See also Wrap Text
Text Box tool, 100
electronic post-it notes
with, 104
Text Color tool, 78
tick marks, 82
in adjusting number
ranges, 96, 97
illustrated, 80
times
changing display of, 9
entering, 33

current, 37
series of, 9
Excel storage of, 34
formats for, 55-56
See also dates
tips, 5-7
chart, 83
for fast text/number
entry, 36-37
toolbar, 22, 46, 76-78, 120,
164
zooming, 22
title bar, 3
illustrated, 4
titles
chart, 88, 94-95
repeating, on every page,
118-119
for rows and columns,
30-31
See also headings
toolbars, 4
adding, 20
Charting, 99
creating custom, 20-21
deciphering, 19
disappearing, 20
Drawing, 100
illustrated, 4
optional, 19
Standard, 4, 6
taking tools off, 21-22
tips for, 22, 46, 76-78, 120,
164
using, 18-20
Utility, 105, 149
tools
assigning macros to, 157,
162-163
chart, 98-100
editing, 76
formatting, 77-78
outline, 149-150
Standard toolbar, 6-7
taking, off toolbar, 21-22
See also specific tools
TrueType fonts, 63

U

unattached text, 95
Utility toolbar, 105

V

values
  adjusting, 50
  copying from above cells,
    37
  See also numbers
Ventura Publisher, 132

W

Window menu, 16, 91
  New Window command,
    137
windows
  application, 3
  document, 3, 137
  workbook contents, 134
Windows, Microsoft, 129-131
Word for Windows, 129, 132
word wrap, 29-30
workbooks, 108
  adding documents to,
    135-136
  closing, 136
  contents window, 134
  creating, 134
  defined, 133
  handling, 135-137
  removing documents
    from, 136
  saving, 134
worksheets, 2-3
  adding/removing from
    edit group, 138
  backup files for, 27
  creating links between,
    122-123
  destination, 122-123, 124,
    130
  embedded charts and, 89
  formatting, 52-66
  function of, 3
  linked
    moving, 124-125
    renaming, 124-125
  moving within, 14-15

multiple, 133-137
  editing, 137-138
names of, 26-27
naming parts of, 5-6
naming regions in, 45
opening existing, 27
saving, 26
sizing, 116
source, 122-123, 124, 130
three parts of, 24
zooming in, 16-17
See also templates;
  workbooks
Wrap Text, 29
  option, 60
  using, 29-30

X

X-axis (categories), 81
  adding labels to, 88
  illustrated, 80
XLM extension, 155
XLSTART directory, 74, 75,
  163
XLW extension, 134

Y

Y-axis (scale), 81
  adding labels to, 88
  adjusting number range
    on, 96-97
  illustrated, 80

Z

Z-axis, 96
zero (0), in number
  formatting, 53, 55, 56
zooming, 16-17
  examples of, 17
  in Print Preview mode,
    110-111
  tips, 22

INDEX

More from Peachpit Press. . .

101 Windows Tips and Tricks
Jesse Berst and Scott Dunn
Compiled by the editors of *Windows Watcher* newsletter, this power-packed, user-friendly survival guide gives you tips and tricks to make Windows faster, easier, and more fun. *(216 pages)*

Desktop Publishing Secrets
Robert Eckhardt, Bob Weibel, and Ted Nace
This is a compilation of hundreds of the best desktop publishing tips from five years of *Publish* magazine. It covers all the major graphics and layout programs on the PC and Macintosh platforms, and valuable tips on publishing as a business. *(550 pages)*

The LaserJet Font Book
Katherine Pfeiffer
A guide to LaserJet fonts and to using type effectively. Hundreds of LaserJet fonts from over a dozen vendors are displayed, accompanied by complete information on price, character sets, and design. *(320 pages)*

The Little DOS 5 Book
Kay Yarborough Nelson
A quick and accessible guide to DOS 5. This book is packed with plenty of tips as well as an easy-to-use section on DOS commands. It also covers DOS basics, working with files and directories, disk management, and more. *(160 pages)*

The Little Windows Book, 3.1 Edition
Kay Yarborough Nelson
This second edition of Peachpit's popular book explains the subtle and not-so-subtle changes in version 3.1 as it gives the essentials of getting started with Windows. Additionally, each chapter includes a handy summary chart of keyboard shortcuts and quick tips. *(144 pages)*

The Little WordPerfect Book
Skye Lininger
Teach yourself the basics of WordPerfect 5.1 in less than an hour. This book gives step-by-step instructions for setting page margins, typing text, navigating with the cursor keys, and more. *(160 pages)*

The Little WordPerfect for Windows Book
Kay Yarborough Nelson
This book gives you the basic skills you need to create simple documents and get familiar with WordPerfect's new Windows interface. *(200 pages)*

PageMaker 4: An Easy Desk Reference
Robin Williams
At last—this highly acclaimed reference book is available for PC users. Here's the book that made Kathy McClelland of *The Page* say, "The book is so superbly indexed and cross-referenced that even if you only halfway know what you're looking for, you'll find it." No serious PageMaker user should be without it. *(768 pages)*

The PC is not a typewriter
Robin Williams
PC users can now learn trade secrets for creating beautiful type, including punctuation, leading, special characters, kerning, fonts, and justification. *(96 pages)*

Ventura Tips and Tricks, 3rd Edition
Ted Nace and Daniel Will-Harris
This book is packed with inside information, speed-up tips, special tricks for reviving a crashed chapter, and ways to overcome memory limitations. Winner of the 1990 Readers' Choice Award from *Publish* magazine. *(790 pages)*

Visual QuickStart Guides (a series)—
- **PageMaker 4.0 (for PC)**
- **Windows 3.1**
- **WordPerfect for Windows**

Webster and Associates

Provides a fast, highly visual introduction to each of these software packages. The Windows and WordPerfect books come with or without tutorial disks.
(approximately 160 pages each)

Winning! The Awesome & Amazing Book of Windows Game Tips, Traps, & Sneaky Tricks

John Hedtke

This book provides rules and explanations for setting up, running, and mastering each game in the Microsoft Entertainment Packs. It includes undocumented tips and anecdotes provided by the programmers themselves on the history and development of the games. Now you can have even more fun with Windows! *(232 pages)*

WordPerfect: Desktop Publishing in Style, 2nd Edition

Daniel Will-Harris

This popular guide (over 90,000 in print) to producing documents with WordPerfect 5.0 or 5.1 opens with a simple tutorial and proceeds through 20 sample documents, each complete with keystroke instructions. Humorous, informative, and delightful to read, this book is invaluable to people who desktop publish with this software program. *(672 pages)*

WordPerfect for Windows with Style

Daniel Will-Harris

This humorous and thoroughly informative handbook gives step-by-step instructions on how to create attractive and effective business documents and promotional materials using WordPerfect for Windows. The book includes valuable insights into styles, graphics, fonts, tables, macros, clip art, printers, and utilities. What's more, it's fun to read. *(528 pages)*

Order Form

(800) 283-9444 or (510) 548-4393
(510) 548-5991 fax

	101 Windows Tips & Tricks	12.95	
	Desktop Publishing Secrets	27.95	
	The LaserJet Font Book	24.95	
	The Little DOS 5 Book	12.95	
	The Little Excel 4 Book, Windows Edition	12.95	
	The Little Windows Book, 3.1 Edition	12.95	
	The Little WordPerfect Book	12.95	
	The Little WordPerfect for Windows Book	12.95	
	PageMaker 4: An Easy Desk Reference (PC Edition)	29.95	
	PageMaker 4: Visual QuickStart Guide (PC Edition)	12.95	
	The PC is not a typewriter	9.95	
	Ventura Tips and Tricks, 3rd Edition	27.95	
	Windows 3.1: Visual QuickStart Guide (with tutorial disk)	24.95	
	Winning!	14.95	
	WordPerfect: Desktop Publishing in Style, 2nd Edition	23.95	
	WordPerfect for Windows with Style	23.95	
	Works for Windows: Visual QuickStart Guide (with disk)	24.95	

Tax of 8.25% applies to California residents only. UPS ground shipping: $4 for first item, $1 each additional. UPS 2nd day air: $7 for first item, $2 each additional. Air mail to Canada: $6 for first item, $4 each additional. Air mail overseas: $14 each item.	Subtotal	
	8.25% Tax (CA only)	
	Shipping	
	TOTAL	

Name		
Company		
Address		
City	State	Zip
Phone	Fax	
❏ Check enclosed	❏ Visa	❏ MasterCard
Company purchase order #		
Credit card #	Expiration Date	

Peachpit Press, Inc. • 2414 Sixth Street • Berkeley, CA • 94710
Your satisfaction is guaranteed or your money will be cheerfully refunded!